SAS
OPERATION GALIA

This book is dedicated to the memory of Stanley William Hann (11th September 1921-5th November 2001) and to all the men who took part in Operation Galia.

Rob Hann 2013

Extract from the SAS Association's Mars and Minerva Review of Galia (2011)

This book contains new material researched by the author and backed by memories of surviving veterans. Galia is not the best known of SAS wartime operations and this book provides insight to it at all levels, from parachutists on the ground to the tactical reasoning with the bigger picture. However, in doing so, the author still manages to retain a personal feel. The author makes no bones that the book was written to understand why his father rarely spoke of his wartime experiences and so that his own children might have a record. This, in itself, is refreshingly honest and his own attempts to walk the Galia escape route through the mountains despite debilitating arthritis, is proof enough of the author's genuine nature. Above all this book is a testament to all members of galia, whether they were SAS, Major Gordon Lett or the local italian population who sheltered, fed and fought alongside members of the Regiment.

General The Lord Guthrie of Craiglebank GCB, LBO, OBE

Rob Hann has made a valuable contribution to the history of the SAS. The exploits of the regiment and its members in italy needed recording in detail and he has achieved this aim admirably. This is an important addition to the SAS story.

Colonel Bob Stewart, DSO, MP for Beckenham

Robert Hann's book on the SAS war service of his father, Stanley Hann, behind enemy lines in the mountains North of La Spezia in Italy is a fascinating account and an intensely interesting read. What particularly attracted me was the way Rob Hann wrote using what he thought to be his father's own voice. This device gave real authenticity to the account and also gave it tremendous atmosphere. Hann was careful to use the language and words of the 1940's which added to this feeling...

All round this book is first-class and contributes hugely to what happened behind enemy lines in Italy. I could not put it down until I had read it from cover to cover and there's not many books that make me do that these days.

Robert Mitchell, Britain at War magazine

SAS Operation galia is an accurate portrayal of this remarkable action. I will be happy to put Rob Hann's excellent publication on the shelves along with my other military history reference books.

SAS
OPERATION GALIA

Bravery behind enemy lines in the

Second World War

Robert Hann

www.fast-print.net/store.php

SAS Operation Galia: Bravery behind enemy
lines in the Second World War
Copyright © Robert Hann 2013

A catalogue record for this book is available from the British Library

ISBN 978-178035-735-5

First published 2013 by
FASTPRINT PUBLISHING
Peterborough, England.

An environmentally friendly book printed and bound in England by
www.printondemand-worldwide.com

Mixed Sources
Product group from well-managed
forests, and other controlled sources
www.fsc.org Cert no. TT-COC-002641
© 1996 Forest Stewardship Council
FSC

PEFC Certified
This product is
from sustainably
managed forests
and controlled
sources
www.pefc.org
PEFC/16-33-415

This book is made entirely of chain-of-custody materials

Contents

About the author

Law, War and the Grumblegroar!

   Rob Hann is a solicitor and Director, Legal Services of a local government specialist procurement agency 'Local Partnerships LLP'. Professionally he has written numerous legal articles and publications as well as two major local government loose-leaf textbooks (Local Authority Companies and Partnerships published by Hann Books Limited and LexisNexis (on-line version) and the PFI and Major Strategic procurement in Local Government' published by Sweet and Maxwell) both of which are regularly updated.

Rob also writes children's rhymes, poetry and stories, one of which 'the Grumblegroar' won the New Writer's UK Children's Book of the Year **(see www.grumblegroarproductions.com)**.

   SAS Operation Galia is Rob's first foray into the non-fiction World War Two genre and his submission, which also formed part of his creative writing MA dissertation at Nottingham Trent University, won the Impress prize for new writers in 2009 and led directly to the publication of the first edition of this book. SAS Operation Galia, second edition, has been published by Hann Books Limited in 2013.

Author's note

What follows is the story I have pieced together since my father's death, using the written records which survive and my own re-collections of conversations or discussions with people connected to or with knowledge of Operation Galia. This includes of course, my late father Stanley 'Spam'Hann, Jimmy Church, Gordon Lett's son, Brian Lett, Ted Robinson and some of the surviving partisan veterans who fought alongside the SAS. Other valuable sources of information have included books on the SAS wartime exploits such as *Stirling's Men* by Gavin Mortimer, *The SAS* by Philip Warner and *Winged Dagger* by SAS 2nd Squadron's war time CO, Major Roy Farran. In 2011, Brian Lett published 'SAS in Tuscany' through Pen and Sword, which, amongst other things, contained new information about some aspects of the Galia Operation not known to me on first publication. Where relevant I have taken the opportunity to correct any significant errors (e.g. captions to photographs) in this second edition but I have not sought to reflect every nuance or difference disclosed.

I hope readers will forgive the literary device I have adopted which is to use my Fathers's 'voice' in the first person as the main narrator to make the story flow. In the final Chapter I have used the voice of my Dad's friend Jimmy Church to relate the story he told me of his dramatic capture and subsequent treatment as a POW, only a few days into Operation Galia. To give the full picture of what happened to various participants when it is clear from the record that my father was not present to witness the events, I have used the voices of Major Lett and Captain Walker Brown to describe what happened to them. These accounts have been distilled from their respective memoirs and reports of Operation Galia, the object being that the events described in this book should be as true to what actually took place as I could make them. This second edition also contains new material contributed by the families of several Galia veterans who have contacted the author since first publication. The Epliogue describes the author's journey of discovery.

This is the story my Dad never told me:

SAS Operation Galia.

Preface

The Italian Campaign 1943–45

The turning of the tide against the Nazis came with a series of Allied victories in 1942–3 and, specifically, with the Battle of Midway in June 1942 when the destruction of four Japanese aircraft carriers abruptly ended Japanese naval superiority in the Pacific. The British-led victory in El Alamein in October and the Allied landings in French North Africa in November, followed by the Axis forces surrender in the desert war, all had an effect. The military catastrophe which eventually engulfed the German Army at Stalingrad in January 1943 effectively ended Nazi expansionist aspirations in the Soviet Union.

By the summer of 1943 the Nazi war machine was looking increasingly vulnerable and was suffering attacks on many fronts as well as a drop in morale after years of constant fighting on foreign soil. German forces suffered another devastating defeat at the hands of the Russians in the great tank battle of Kursk. German cities were also being attacked from the air on a regular basis by British and American bombers; Japan was suffering unsustainable losses of aircraft and merchant shipping.

The fortunes of the various resistance groups which had been established began to improve, with the help of clandestine Allied support through such organisations as the Special Operations Executive (SOE).

The **Special Operations Executive** (**SOE**) was initiated by Prime Minister Winston Churchill and Minister of Economic Warfare Hugh Dalton on July 22, 1940, to conduct warfare by means other than direct military engagement. Its mission was to encourage and facilitate espionage and sabotage behind enemy lines and to serve as the core of the Auxiliary Units, a British resistance movement.

It was also known as 'Churchill's Secret Army' and was charged by Churchill to 'set Europe ablaze'.

In the aftermath of the Italian capitulation in 1943, the SOE helped build a large resistance organisation in the cities of northern Italy, and in the Alps. Italian partisans harassed German forces in Italy throughout the autumn and winter of 1944–5.

The SOE established a base at Bari in Southern Italy, from which they operated their networks and agents thoughout Europe and the Balkans.

Some partisan groups in France, Northern Italy (as we shall see) and Yugoslavia by the latter stages of the war had blossomed to become strong military forces. The communist factions in particular became very active in many places. This also complicated the situation in some areas, particularly Italy, since the objective of the communists was often to encourage revolution after overcoming the immediate threat posed by the fascist forces currently ranged against them. This sometimes prevented co-ordinated opposition to the common enemy.

Mussolini

Italy had a short history as a single nation, and its politics had always been diverse. Benito Mussolini founded his Fascist Party in 1919 as a militant, anti-socialist movement. He ruled Italy from 1922 and by 1925 he had fully established his position as dictator. His career was followed with great interest by Adolf Hitler as he similarly rose from obscurity to absolute power and dictatorship in the 1930s. By then Mussolini and his fascist state had, seemingly, brought long overdue modernisation to Italy and had instilled in the wider population a sense of national pride which (like Germany) had been dented by its performance in the First World War. The effectiveness and impact of Italian fascism was limited and curtailed to an extent by the power of the Roman Catholic Church. Gradually, Mussolini became more and more influenced by his charismatic German counterpart. In 1937, Hitler persuaded Mussolini to sign the anti-commiturn pact which further strengthened the bond between the two fascist heads of state by expressing their common antipathy for communism.

For many ordinary hard-working Italians and their families, in particular the *contadini* (peasants), the fascist state was simply a fact of life, to be tolerated, much like the weather, sometimes good, sometimes bad. To most mountain folk, central government in any form was generally despised and its taxes disliked. Many youngsters joined the Fascist movement simply as a convenient youth club, without giving any particular thought to the aims or real meaning of Fascism. Each town and village would have its identifiable fascists, but they would generally be relatively few, busying themselves with politics and self-aggrandisement, whilst the rest of the population got on with the daily grind of making a living. It was only when Mussolini decided to go to war that the situation began to change.

Mussolini, like Hitler, undoubtedly had grandiose plans to establish Italy as a major world power, but unlike Hitler he didn't plan to achieve his ends by provoking a major war involving his European neighbours. Instead he preferred smaller adventures, where the stakes were not so high, where the world's attention was perhaps not as focused and where his better-equipped forces stood a good chance of overwhelming a weaker, less well-equipped opposition. The invasion of Abyssinia in 1935–6 typifies his approach.

Mussolini, whilst signing a formal alliance (the so called 'Pact of Steel') with Hitler in 1939, was also cautious about declaring his wholehearted support for Germany's war aims. When Britain and France declared war with Germany in September 1939 Mussolini preferred to wait and see how events transpired before showing his true allegiances, declaring Italy a 'non-belligerent' state. Only when France and most of Europe had fallen to Hitler and the Nazis in June 1940 and Britain looked certain to follow, did Mussolini finally determine that the time was ripe to declare himself and his country on the side of what he must have thought at that time would be the obvious ultimate victor. Mussolini was concerned that Italy would risk missing out on the spoils of war following Hitler's surprisingly rapid advance through north-west Europe

Italy thus entered into the conflict, allied to Germany, on the 10th June 1940 and as a 'reward' Hitler permitted Italy to occupy two small pieces of territory in Southern France, following that country's capitulation. However, this was not sufficient to satisfy Mussolini's ambition and he ordered his forces to invade Greece in October.

This proved a disastrous adventure for the Italians and their forces were soon swept back by the Allies into Albania by the end of the year. Italian forces proved similarly ill-prepared for battle and suffered heavy losses whilst fighting the British in North and East Africa. Importantly, many ordinary Italian servicemen felt a natural affinity towards the British and Americans, and had relatives living and working in the United Kingdom or the US, and had no wish to fight against them. The orders of their fascist leaders failed to create any *esprit de corps* or great enthusiasm for the conflict.

Germany was soon forced to come to the assistance of the Italians in both theatres of war (Greece and Africa) instigated by Mussolini, but not before a large part of his Mediterranean fleet had been destroyed by the Allies. Only the Italian midget submarines proved to be a real success.

By the summer of 1943, following a string of military defeats in Africa, Albania, Greece, Egypt, Libya and Tunisia, the Allied invasion of Sicily and Allied bombing raids on the Italian mainland, industrial strikes in Milan and Turin had plunged Italy into political chaos. Hitler was so concerned upon hearing reports that the Italian Army was in a state of collapse that he made a lightening visit to Northern Italy to bolster his friend's morale. He promised to provide Mussolini with reinforcements, U-boats and new terror weapons in return for Italy's continued support. But Mussolini's downfall was near. Arriving back from his meeting with Hitler he found Rome had been bombed by the Allies and rebellion was in the air.

On the 25th July 1943, Mussolini was placed under arrest and formally stripped of office by King Victor Emmanuel III, having being voted out by his former supporters on the ruling 'Fascist Grand Council'. It was 'Finito Benito', as the British Officer's at Chieti POW camp's Information Agency were to put it.

The king took control of the armed forces and appointed an anti-fascist, Marshal Pietro Badoglio, as Prime Minister. From then on, Italy searched for an exit strategy from the war but that proved very difficult to achieve.

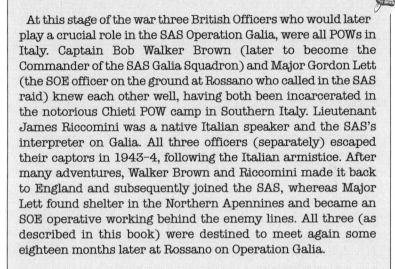

At this stage of the war three British Officers who would later play a crucial role in the SAS Operation Galia, were all POWs in Italy. Captain Bob Walker Brown (later to become the Commander of the SAS Galia Squadron) and Major Gordon Lett (the SOE officer on the ground at Rossano who called in the SAS raid) knew each other well, having both been incarcerated in the notorious Chieti POW camp in Southern Italy. Lieutenant James Riccomini was a native Italian speaker and the SAS's interpreter on Galia. All three officers (separately) escaped their captors in 1943-4, following the Italian armistice. After many adventures, Walker Brown and Riccomini made it back to England and subsequently joined the SAS, whereas Major Lett found shelter in the Northern Apennines and became an SOE operative working behind the enemy lines. All three (as described in this book) were destined to meet again some eighteen months later at Rossano on Operation Galia.

The Allies had landed in Sicily at Syracuse on the 10th July 1943 and liberated the island as a prelude to the full-scale invasion of the Italian mainland which took place two months later. However, despite Mussolini's overthrow, the Italian's were still technically at war with the Allies. At the same time, Italy itself was playing 'host' to significant numbers of German forces.

This must have been a time of great danger and confusion for many Italians. Their erstwhile German allies, who had come to their assistance when they had got themselves into trouble in Greece and Africa, now regarded them with distain and disgust as it looked increasingly likely that Italy would attempt to extricate itself from the war. In early August 1943 the Italian Government assured the Germans there would be no separate peace negotiations with the Allies but, following a devastating Allied bombing raid on Milan on the 12th August, secret negotiations for an armistice began. General Giuseppe Castellano was despatched to the newly liberated island of Sicily to seek whatever assurances he could from the Allies that they would assist the Italian people to resist reprisals from the German occupying forces within Italy, in return for Italy's cessation from hostilities. On the 3rd September General Castellano signed an agreement to cease hostilities with the Allies, and to delay an announcement of the armistice, so as not to prejudice the imminent Allied invasion plans which were about to be put into action at Salerno.

Although General Castellano had hoped to sign his country out of the war, unfortunately this depended upon the Germans doing the 'decent thing' by withdrawing from Italy. Of course they did not do so. The Germans generally showed no inclination to yield territory without heavy fighting and in Italy they acted true to form, by promptly moving to occupy Rome and to re-enforce other vital strategic positions. The Royalist Government in the South then declared war on Germany.

As events were to prove over the next two years, the liberation of Italy became one of the hardest and bitterly fought campaigns of the war, very costly in terms of casualties, both civilian and military, and lasting right up to the death-throes of the Third Reich. To complicate matters further, once it became clear that eventually the Allies would win the war, the political competition between the various partisan bands operating in enemy-occupied Italy became intense. Political activists looked beyond the increasingly inevitable fall of Mussolini to the political vacuum that would exist thereafter. After so many years of dictatorship, this was perhaps both understandable and inevitable, but it proved on occasion an appreciable handicap to British and American missions and operations behind enemy lines.

The formation of the SAS

The origins of the Special Air Service began in 1941 when a young Lieutenant in the Scots Guards called David Stirling had a bright idea while recuperating in hospital from injuries sustained on his first parachute jump. The plan he came up with involved the establishment of small highly mobile and highly trained units of men who would operate far behind enemy lines in order to exploit the element of surprise to the full. The object would be to disrupt enemy communications and supply lines and generally to cause as much mayhem as possible for the enemy before slipping away.

Stirling argued that a small force focused on a strategically important target such as an aerodrome, roads, fuel depot or vehicles would cause the enemy real problems but with minimal demands on manpower, equipment and resources. Moreover, the destruction of fifty aircraft or units of transport was, he reckoned, more easily accomplished by a sub-unit of five men than by a force of 200.

He proposed each unit must be self-sufficient and responsible for its own training and operational planning and that forty such units be recruited in the first instance and trained to arrive on the scene by land, sea or air as the occasion demanded. Stirling, as a relatively junior ranked officer, had to show great initiative to get his proposals before the relevant army 'Top Brass' and turn his bright idea into reality – but initiative was a resource Stirling had in spades.

Two days after getting his proposals in a most unorthodox way, before General Claude Auchinleck, the then new Commander-in-Chief of the Middle East, Stirling was promoted to captain and given a brief to recruit six officers and sixty men for a force to be known as L Detachment, Special Air Service Brigade. Based at Kabrit near the Suez Canal, Stirling began his recruitment drive drawing on volunteers from the commando forces, the men who subsequently became known as the 'Originals'. After three months of training, during which two men were killed when their parachutes failed to open, and after his men had carried out successful 'dummy raids' against an RAF airfield, L Detachment SAS was ready for action.

By then they had been given their unique identity – the winged dagger cap badge and their motto 'Who Dares Wins' – and had been briefed on their first operation. Planned for November 1941, to coincide with a British offensive codenamed Operation Crusader, Stirling and his men were supposed to hit five airfields on the North African coast and blow up as many enemy aircraft on the ground as they could before the British offensive began. The day of the parachute drop the weather intervened. Despite strong winds the five planes took off carrying the SAS force.

As they neared the drop zone two planes were shot down by anti-aircraft fire and of the three units that successfully managed to jump into the gale, most were blown off course. A number of these men were injured on landing and to compound the problems, the bombs they had brought were recovered but not the detonators. Without them the mission had to be abandoned and in bedraggled groups the survivors made their way to the rendezvous where they were to be met and picked up by the Long Range Desert Group (a British reconnaissance and intelligence gathering unit) in their Chevrolet trucks. Only 22 of the original 65 men were in the event collected by the LRDG.

However, from this inauspicious start, Stirling drew one positive conclusion which was to serve the SAS well in the remainder of their North African Desert campaign: if the LRDG could get his men out, they could also get them within walking distance of their targets and there was no need to risk the uncertainties and inherent dangers of parachute drops in order to commence operations.

In December 1941 the remaining 'Originals' launched frequent surprise attacks against enemy airfields behind the lines at numerous sites and successfully destroyed over 100 enemy aircraft plus stores, petrol and vehicles. Their tactics proved a great success in the desert and the SAS was responsible for destroying more enemy aircraft on the ground than the RAF destroyed in the air.

With success came the need for more recruits and L Detachment was increased to two troops of 60 men. Throughout the summer of 1942 these units attacked airfields and harried road traffic in small raiding parties across the North African Front.

In September the SAS was raised to full regimental status – 1 SAS Regiment – with an HQ squadron and four combat squadrons – A, B, the Free French and the Special Boat Squadron (SBS), the latter two know as C and D respectively. By December Lieutenant Colonel Stirling (as he now was) had over 650 men under his command and the new year began well for the British: Rommel was in full retreat after El Alamein and the SAS was launching ever more hit and run attacks on the enemy troops as they retreated.

But then Stirling was captured after accompanying his men on a sabotage mission behind enemy lines in North Africa towards the end of January 1943.

Stirling's capture led to the break up of the original SAS with the Free French and Greeks who had joined going back to their respective armies and the maritime section, the SBS, hived off to Palestine. The 250 strong 1 SAS was renamed the Special Raiding Squadron ('SRS'). However, the Stirling family were a resourceful bunch and David's brother Bill had, in the meantime, created another SAS regiment – 2 SAS – which had fought with great distinction in the Allied invasions of Sicily and Italy in 1943. Success required the ranks of the SAS to be constantly refreshed and renewed and 2 SAS carried out a further recruitment campaign in the autumn of 1943 to establish 3 Squadron.

The Allied invasion of Italy

General Eisenhower (the Supreme Allied Commander) announced the Italian surrender on the 8th September 1943, timed to coincide with the major Allied landings on the west coast of Italy at Salerno and to avoid resistance by Italian troops stationed on the coast. The German response to the news was swift and they took action to repel the Allied forces and prevent them from establishing a beachhead.

The Germans had realised well in advance of the armistice what was likely to happen. Italy had lost Sicily to the Allies, Mussolini had been deposed and confined to a mountain prison, and inevitably the new government would look to sue for peace. Germany could not afford to give up Italy without a fight, since Italy could never now be a non-military zone, and an Allied presence there would expose Germany to attack from a mainland foothold to its south. Germany had to fight for Italy in order to maintain its own security. Therefore, in the weeks before the armistice it increased its military presence in Italy, and prepared for the worst.

Within weeks of Mussolini's arrest he was rescued from his mountain top prison, a hotel on top of the Gran Sasso D'Italia, the highest range in the Abruzzi Apennines. The hotel could only be reached over land by funicular railway. The Germans learned of Mussolini's whereabouts, made aerial reconnaissance and decided that glider troops might make a landing, overcome the *Carabinieri* and could escape with the *Duce* in a small plane. Incredibly, this daring plan was carried out on September 13th under the leadership of an SS officer called Otto Skorzeny.

As soon as he was rescued, Hitler appointed his old friend Mussolini as a puppet ruler in the northern part of Italy that Germany still occupied . . . no longer 'Finito Benito'.

Mussolini's fascist supporters kept him in power for a further eighteen months in that part of Italy yet to be liberated by the Allies. Mussolini used the *Brigata Nera*, the Fascist Militia, in conjunction with the Waffen-SS and the Gestapo, to instil terror into those who showed dissent to his rule. For the first time Jews were deported from Italy into Germany where they faced Hitler's Final Solution.

The German forces in Italy had the good fortune to be commanded by a military leader of great resilience and fortitude in the person of Field Marshal Kesselring. In consequence, Allied progress, even with the great advantage of overwhelming air supremacy, was painfully slow. Kesselring master-minded a strategy designed to slow down or prevent the Allied advance through Italy. He ordered the building of a series of formidable defensive lines, the first of which was established south of Rome. Known as the Gustav Line, it ran from coast to coast, and included the stronghold mountain fortress of Monte Cassino.

The country along the Gustav Line was rugged and difficult to traverse. The winter weather in 1944–5 was bitter, one of the worst in living memory. The German troops were tough, battle-hardened and experienced. It was a feature, also, of German/fascist tactics that they used the utmost brutality to suppress any signs of resistance. Kesselring was to (in part) answer for this at Nuremberg in the post-war reckoning for sanctioning some of the most brutal atrocities carried out against civilians in the west.[1] Anyone suspected of helping the thousands of escaped prisoners of war who were filtering south to meet the Allied advance was summarily executed. On occasions, whole villages were massacred, such as at Pietransieri in the Abruzzo region. War crimes were commonplace. Despite these obstacles, it was through this line, in its very early days, that many allied ex-POWs escaped from their captors to try to make it back across the Allied lines, including Captain Bob Walker Brown and Lieutenant James Riccomini who would later both take part in SAS Operation Galia.

The Gustav defensive line held the Allies from the autumn of 1943 until May 1944, when the Germans, after fierce battles and much bloodshed on both sides, finally abandoned Monte Cassino and withdrew further north.

The Allied liberation of Rome took place on the 4th/5th June 1944, but this event was soon eclipsed by events taking place the very next day. On the 6th June, the Allies launched their long-awaited invasion of France. Accordingly, the world's attention switched to this theatre of war along with a considerable amount of the Allied manpower, weaponry and resources needed to sustain the Italian offensive. As a result, troops remaining in Italy shared with the 14th Army in Burma the feeling that they were the 'forgotten army'. By the summer of 1944, the Axis forces fell back to entrench along another defensive position known as the Gothic Line. This line had been constructed a short distance south of the major naval port of La Spezia, below the Magra valley. The line was in fact two lines, one the front line, and the other mainly an artillery line higher up on the mountain ridges, with a good command of the coastal plain along which all traffic had to travel.

Kesselring had, once again, wisely chosen a natural defensive position, running across the entire width of Italy, to help with his strategy of holding up further Allied advances through the country. Here, the Nazis and their fascist supporters adopted ruthless terror tactics to try to subdue any sympathy for the Allies amongst the local population. There were a number of massacres, including one at the village of Vinca, which stood at the gateway to the Marble Mountains of Carrara, and was an important staging point on the supply route to the Gothic Line.

In December 1944 Hitler ordered a major counter-offensive in the Ardennes region of Belgium, which came as a huge shock to the Allied forces in the area. The offensive became known as the 'Battle of the Bulge' and, at one point, came perilously close to breaking through the Allied lines and succeeding in its objectives.

---

1   Although the death sentence was commuted to life imprisonment and commuted again so he was released in 1952. He died in 1960.

At the same time, on the Gothic Line in Northern Italy, Allied commanders in the field became increasingly worried about the ability of their forces to resist a similar concerted counter-attack at certain points along that front where experienced, battle hardened Allied troops, weapons, food and ammunition were in very short supply. Emergency measures were needed to address the drastic situation the Allies faced and to take the pressure off the beleaguered front-line forces. A plan was hurriedly put together. For a squadron of highly trained paratroopers attached to the Special Air Service, Christmas was cancelled.

SAS Operation Galia was about to begin.

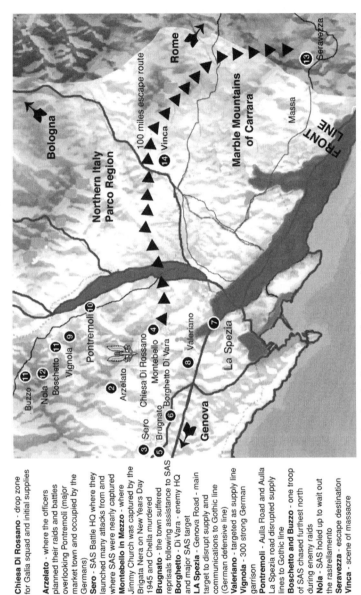

Map showing the drop zone, key targets, battle ground and the approximate escape route used by the men of SAS Operation Galia

1 **Chiesa Di Rossano** - drop zone for Galia squad and initial supplies

2 **Arzelato** - where the officers planned their raids and battles overlooking Pontremoli (major market town and occupied by the Germans)

3 **Sero** - SAS Battle HQ where they launched many attacks from and where SAS were nearly captured

4 **Montebello in Mezzo** - where Jimmy Church was captured by the Brigata Nera on New Years Day 1945 and Chella murdered

5 **Brugnato** - the town suffered reprisals following assistance to SAS

6 **Borghetto** - Di Vara - enemy HQ and major SAS target

7 **LA Spezia** - Genova Road - main target to disrupt supply and communications to Gothic line (German defensive line)

8 **Valeriano** - targeted as supply line

9 **Vignola** - 300 strong German garrison

10 **Pontremoli** - Aulla Road and Aulla La Spezia road disrupted supply lines to Gothic line

11 **Boschetto and Buzzo** - one troop of SAS chased furthest north during enemy raids

12 **Nola** - SAS holed up to wait out the rastrellamento

13 **Seravezza** - escape destination

14 **Vinca** - scene of massacre

▲ ESCAPE ROUTE

PART ONE
Operation Galia

Me, with a Corporal's stripe, 1945.

Chapter 1
In the beginning

'What did you do in the war, Dad?'

You used to ask me that all the time. I told you about the laughs I had with my mates when we went through selection and basic training for the parachute jumps.

I never told you about 'Galia'. We were sworn to secrecy about Operations in the Special Air Service (SAS) and as soon as the war was over, the Regiment was disbanded. We all went our separate ways.

Why?

Well, Top Brass never liked us for one thing. We didn't fit in. Glory hunters, they said. Too bloody insubordinate more like. Didn't do as we were told. Didn't march about in shiny boots or salute and say 'Yes Sir, No Sir, Three bags full Sir' to any fancy dan officer who happened to be passing. We did things differently in the SAS. The officers and men trained together and there was no standing on ceremony.

By the time you came along it didn't seem that relevant any more. It was different world. I was 19 when I joined up in 1940 and 25 when de-mobbed. For my generation, the war stole the best years of our lives. We made the best of it at the time but what we went through wasn't pleasant and I didn't want to glorify it. The last thing I wanted was to encourage my boys to join the forces or for you to think war is like it is portrayed in the movies. Besides, everyone did something back then. You know, 'did their bit' as we used to say.

After it was all over there were many like me who just wanted to forget about it and move on.

It seems odd now, but no-one outside those who needed to know had heard of the SAS. We didn't shout about our existence. The hostage rescue following the Iranian Embassy siege in 1980 brought the Regiment to the public's attention but those lads were very different from our lot. They were professional soldiers for one thing. We were all just ordinary blokes, picked to do an odd sort of job in extra-ordinary times.

I never wanted to be a soldier. I never wanted to fire weapons or jump out of planes and I never wanted to kill anyone. Only two years before I joined up I'd been a milkman, doing my rounds every morning delivering milk to the swanky houses on Winchmore Hill. I was the youngest of six, crowded into one floor of a Victorian tenement in Tottenham. My dad died when I was 11. I had to leave school at 14 to provide for my mum and sisters.

A dairy rounds-man's job (to give it its posh title) suited me down to the ground. I went back to being a 'milky' after the war. You and your brothers helped me on round as kids, remember? The sunny, summer mornings; the dawn chorus; tea and toast with the regulars. Up every morning at 4.30 am come rain or shine and loading up the cart. We didn't get electric milk floats until the 1960s. Hurricane – Home Counties' finest – pulled the cart along in those days. He would trot slowly up and down the road as good as gold all morning but the nearer we got to the end of the round, the faster he cantered. He knew his oats were waiting back at the stable. On the final stretch it would take all my strength to reign the bugger back.

When Hitler came along, of course, everything changed. We couldn't sit back and let him bomb our cities, murder civilians and invade our country. We had to do something. Hard to credit it now, but back then, being a milky had made me as fit as a fiddle and virtually immune to anything the weather could throw at me. Enough to get me through SAS basic training.

Not that I joined them straight away. When I got my call up papers I spent my first year in the army attached to an anti-aircraft battery on the North Lincolnshire coast. We scoured the skies day after day for enemy aircraft. On the rare occasions we saw any, we had next to no chance of hitting them. I was bored stiff.

One day, I think it was around autumn 1943, a sign went up in the mess. It said anyone wanting to join a new 'special force' comprised entirely of volunteers should sign up. An extra shilling a week was offered as incentive. A shilling was worth having in those days and anything was better than what I was doing at that time, or so I thought.

I passed the medical with no problems although they said at 5'9" I was a bit on the short side. We were put through our paces on the assault course. The instructors, bless them, loaded our Bergen back packs with bricks weighing up to 90 pounds. The bricks were stamped so we couldn't cheat and drop them out on the sly. Those who couldn't hack it were RTU'd (returned to unit). Quite a few were weeded out like that.

Those remaining then had to get through the selection board. The recruiters were looking for fit, tough customers who could think for and look after themselves, who could maintain the integrity of the unit and keep quiet about its activities. They didn't want gung-ho, loud mouthed mavericks, drunken, brawling thugs, glory hunters or (at the other extreme) 'shrinking violets'.

The first thing that struck me as a new recruit was the informality. The absence of clean and tidy uniforms. No drills, polishing shoes, marching or saluting officers every five minutes. There was an unusual, more relaxed atmosphere between SAS officers, NCOs and other ranks. The officers and NCOs had to earn the respect of the men and although there was a healthy regard for rank, there were very few 'Hooray Henries' or 'toffee-nosed' public school types in the SAS upper echelons. Those who did get through were there on merit and had to live up to their billing.

I met your 'Uncle' Jim after we'd both made it through initial recruitment. Jimmy Church was a big, stocky bloke, around six feet tall, strong as an ox, with a chiseled 'Desperate Dan' chin. He'd been apprenticed as a stevedore before the war, on the docks in Bermondsey. A real cockney. Like me, Jimmy came from a big family but his mum died a couple of years before the war. He volunteered for the services as soon as war was declared in 1939. Jimmy was 17 when he joined up and lied about his age to enlist. There was only one thing Jimmy was scared of – flying. He told me that's why he'd volunteered for the SAS – so he could have a parachute and jump out when he'd had enough.

We both palled up with Eric Kennedy around that time. Kennedy was very tall and thin, over 6'4". Gaunt and gangly, 'all knees and elbows', we said. Inevitably, he was re-christened 'Lofty'.

But Kennedy wasn't his real name. There were many foreign nationals in the SAS including South Africans, French, Belgians and Poles, all of whom had joined up under the British flag to fight the Nazis. Kennedy though, belonged to a group of German speakers in the squad, known as the 'funnies'. He came from Austria, spoke English with a German accent. Not the best attribute to have in the forces at that time. He and those like him got a lot of stick as you can imagine but he had a great sense of humour and took all the ribbing in good heart. We found out years later that he was part Jewish and his father had got him out of Austria just before the Nazi Anschluss in

1938. The rest of his family were not so fortunate.

One of Lofty's endearing features was that he was always getting into scrapes. Soon after we met, me, Jimmy and Lofty were on leave at Jimmy's house in Bermondsey. During a *Luftwaffe* bombing raid on the docks, Kennedy, wearing his SAS uniform and winged dagger beret dashed out of the Anderson shelter, jumped on the roof and started to shout and swear in German at the bombers, explosions going off all around him. Before we could drag him back the police nabbed him, not unreasonably believing the strangely clad, gangly, German-speaking parachutist was a downed enemy pilot. He was lucky not to have been lynched on the spot. It took all our combined powers of persuasion to convince the constabulary that Kennedy was on our side and was a member of the British Army's elite Parachute Squadron.

Kennedy was also what you might call 'accident prone'. He got shot twice in separate training incidents, before ever getting near a plane. Neither incident caused serious injury. Incident one was courtesy of Jimmy Church who had been cleaning his pistol after firing practice but had left a round in the breach. A shot went off and suddenly Kennedy's hopping around the firing range. Jimmy had shot off the tip of Lofty's big toe. Jimmy got put on a charge for that and had his pay docked for two weeks. He wasn't best pleased.

The second incident came a month or two later. I was leading a patrol on manoeuvres in the Scottish highlands. As we crossed a field and climbed over a style there was a loud 'Bang!'

I turned to the trooper behind me, Lofty Kennedy.

'What was that? Sounded like a shot?'

Kennedy tried to shrug his shoulders but a smoking hole on one side prevented him from doing so. Lofty managed to say something like 'Sheissa! I've shot me bloody self'. Then his face went white and he passed out – cold.

We got him to hospital somehow where he stayed for a couple of weeks, having a nice time of it initially. The nurses made a big fuss of him. They all assumed he had been wounded in action. When we got back the Commander actually complimented me on the 'sterling job' we had done getting 'the casualty' to hospital. Until, that is, he realised it was for real and wasn't part of the exercise simulation. I lost my corporal's stripe since I was the patrol leader and that didn't endear me to Kennedy either. When we saw all the fuss the nurses were making of him in hospital, Jimmy, somewhat uncharitably 'had a word', intimating to the nurses that Kennedy's wound had been self-inflicted. Poor Kennedy never did find out why his popularity plummeted so soon after our visit.

Somehow me, Jimmy and Kennedy (despite his wounds) managed to get through the medical, the selection board, the assault course and survival training. Only parachute training awaited, at Ringway Aerodrome near Manchester.

Parachuting was still in its relative infancy in 1943. The army had been experimenting to find the most realistic way of training recruits. To be honest, we were all apprehensive about our first proper parachute jump although no-one would ever admit it. We never went near a plane in those first few weeks. We had to practise how to jump, land and roll safely from specially constructed wooden platforms, set on trolleys. The training soon became more realistic, albeit somewhat rudimentary. We had to jump and roll from the tail-gait of a truck moving around 20–30 mph. There were several relatively minor casualties from that exercise and even the odd broken bone or two. I was lucky. Not a scratch.

By far the most terrifying element of training was the jump from the static barrage balloons. A large wicker basket was suspended beneath the balloons and a steel hawser connected the basket to a winch on the back of a lorry. We climbed up into the basket which was then winched into the air. The winching stopped when the basket was in position about 700 feet up. What spooked us most was the absolute silence as we waited our turn to leap off the edge into oblivion. In a plane, at least the noise and roar of the engines drown out everything else, including thoughts and fears.

Basket and occupants swayed in the breeze until the novice plucked up sufficient courage to launch himself into space, sometimes with a little 'help' from the hard faced instructor. We regarded all instructors as a particular low form of pond life. They thought they were born comedians. They knew there would be a four second delay and a fall of about 200 feet before the parachute canopy opened – a major difference between a balloon and an aircraft jump. The instructor's took full advantage:

'Come back here you silly bastard. You're not hooked up!' Were often the last words the terrified novice would hear as he plummeted to Earth. Invariably, a few seconds later, with the canopy safely deployed, the 'psychotic' instructors' maniacal laughter would accompany the unfortunate recruit all the way to the ground.

No second chance, remember. No reserve chutes in those days. If the parachute was packed wrongly, the rigging lines got tangled up or the canopy didn't open . . . we called them 'Roman candles' – a few of the lads copped it that way during operations but none, thankfully, at Ringway while we were there.

The first 'proper' jump most of us did was from a specially adapted Whitley bomber. We christened the Whitley's 'flying coffins'. We hated them. The fuselage was not designed for passengers of any kind, let alone battle-ready parachutists with packs on their backs and weapon bags. We had to crawl on our hands and knees into the dark, narrow fuselage tunnel and then sit cross legged on the floor waiting for take-off. The Whitleys could only take ten, maximum. Five on each side of a small hole in the fuselage floor which had been thoughtfully added to allow us some means of exiting the aircraft when the time was right. I preferred being on the forward side. Those unfortunate to be lined up 'aft' had their legs blasted back by the slip-stream on their way out. As the body pivoted, their faces would get smashed against the hard edge of the hole. We called it 'ringing the bell' – broken noses and black eyes were commonplace.

We didn't have ripcords to open our parachutes at the time of our choosing. Instead, we had a thin strap called the static line which had to be securely clipped to a strong point in the aircraft before we jumped out. Provided the static line was attached properly to the rail that ran down the centre ceiling of the Whitley, the parachute canopy would be automatically deployed as soon as we left the aircraft. All it took when the green light came on was enough 'bottle' to leap through the trap door into the freezing empty space below and trust that the line would safely tug the canopy out of the parachute bag strapped to our backs.

What worried me most was how I would react when it was my turn to jump. Anyone who refused had to keep his pack on his back when he got off the plane so that everyone could see he had 'chickened out'. Men who refused the first time were generally given a second chance but were returned to unit (RTU'd) if they failed the next time.

I remember my first jump. As soon as I leapt through the hole, the down-draft buffeted me from all sides like a playground bully. Almost immediately, as I tumbled away from the Whitley, the canopy pulled free of the bag and mushroomed out above my head. For a few precious moments, I hung onto the harness and looked around, exhilarated. I felt more alive in those few moments than at any time in my entire life.

Then I looked down.

Green and brown fields seemed to be accelerating towards me. I bent my knees ready to take the shock of landing as I'd been taught. The impact shook the breath from my body and I rolled and rolled as the NCO reception committee barked out instructions:

'Tuck those knees and elbows in you 'orrible specimen! Right, now. Bloody well get up and stop larkin' about. Roll up your chute and bugger off before your mate lands on yer 'ead.'

Groggily, I got to my feet, just in time to see, first, Jimmy Church, and then the gangly figure of Lofty Kennedy landing safely behind me. True to form, Kennedy had obviously succeeded in 'ringing the bell' on his exit from the Whitley. A thin trail of blood ran down his aquiline nose from a cut on his forehead but Kennedy was sporting the biggest grin I had ever seen as he unclipped his parachute from the harness and ran towards me and Jimmy, punching the air triumphantly.

Our first proper parachute jump. We had made it through the final ordeal of SAS basic training. Only another seven jumps to go to earn our parachute wings.

Me, Stanley Hann, and my mother, Clara, in 1944.

The need for SAS Operation Galia

Following the German surprise counter-offensive in Belgium, Allied commanders on the ground in Italy became increasingly concerned that a similar concerted attack might be repeated on the Italian front. The loosely defended 1V Corps sector above Leghorn and Pisa appeared particularly vulnerable to a determined enemy attack. The rugged Apuan Alps front was lightly defended on both sides.

Allied command could see that the Tyrrhenian coastal plain and the Serchio valley made natural shooting galleries for a pincer movement aimed at Leghorn. If the port was recaptured by the enemy and lost to the Allies, it would have become impossible to adequately supply the 5th Army in the vastness of the Apennines. Leghorn was defended by only one division, the 92nd, which was under US Army command. Their available forces were widely extended across a broad front and divided on opposite sides of the 13-mile mountainous Apuan Massif. Moreover 1V Corps had no reserves to re-enforce the line. Other theatres of war in France, Belgium, Holland and elsewhere were thirstily soaking up any available fresh troops, supplies and equipment.

Intelligence reports from the partisans operating in the mountains warned of enemy troop movements and frequent attacks in force on the partisan formations operating there. Bridges and roads in strategically important positions were being cleared and rebuilt by enemy forces. Aerial photographs confirmed the Allies' worst fears, namely that the Germans were securing their supply lines in readiness for a major attack along the Gothic Line.

Before action could be taken by the Allies, the Germans seized the initiative. On the 18th December a concerted attack took place on the 6th Partisan Zone, which comprised the whole area to the north west as far as Genoa. The partisans bravely resisted the enemy forces for three days but were eventually forced to disperse into the mountains. An undercover American mission, code-named 'Wala Wala', which had been operating in the area until this attack, was forced to escape through the Rossano valley to avoid capture. The partisans also reported that the enemy were gathering in force to the north-east preparing for a further *rastrellamento* (a raking through of enemy forces to locate and destroy partisans and terrorise the inhabitants). The estimate of enemy troops active in the region included a division of the 148 Panzer Grenadiers, two Italian Fascist Alpine regiments, the 16th SS Recce Battalion supported by specialist Mongolian Alpine Divisions equipped with skis and snow suits. Only the 4th Partisan Zone (the Rossano valley) had so far not been attacked. The partisans here, though, were surrounded by enemy forces. Intelligence indicated this area would be the next to suffer a similar fate.

The anticipated attack on American Allied lines came when the German Division holding the right of the Gothic Line mounted what it later described as a 'reconnaissance in strength' to probe for weaknesses in the Allied line. The 5th US Army, courtesy of the 91st Negro Division were holding the Allied left, but following concerted enemy attacks and a lack of adequate rein-forcements, ammunition and supplies, these positions were abandoned. The British 8th Indian Division were mobilised and moved up to prevent further enemy exploitation and to re-enforce the line but this was an emergency measure and not a long-term solution which ideally needed to be resolved by a substantial injection of fresh troops. The trouble was such resources were not available to the beleaguered 5th Army. Allied forces were stretched across all fronts in France, Belgium and Northern Italy where the American-led forces were bogged down by the deteriorating weather conditions and the tenacious fighting of the well-entrenched German defenders. Consequently, the threat to the hard-won positions on this flank of the Allied side of the Gothic Line remained perilous, subject to enemy exploitation and breakthrough any day unless a counter-strategy could be devised to take some of the pressure off.

At the Allied High Command in Italy just such a counter-strategy was being worked up and hurriedly organised. For some time, a British SOE operative, codenamed *Blundell Violett,* working in secret behind the enemy lines in the valley of Rossano, had been recommending to base commanders in Florence that his current position, deep in the mountains above and behind the German defensive positions on the Gothic Line, would be an ideal place to launch a surprise offensive against the enemy, from a position they would least expect an attack to come. *Blundell Violett* was the *nom de guerre* of ex-POW escapee Major Gordon Lett who had been living in the mountains and had trained a guerrilla army of partisan volunteers known as the International Battalion. Major Lett was convinced that if such a force was to have any chance of success, an operation needed to take place before his Rossano base was overrun by the enemy. He suggested a force of up to 300 paratroopers be dropped into the valley to link up with his partisan forces.

By co-ordinating and combining trained commandos with highly motivated local forces who knew the rugged terrain, ground conditions and best attacking positions, Major Lett anticipated enemy forces would be forced to defend themselves and launch search and destroy missions which would, in turn, put strain on the front-line forces and prevent or delay further enemy offensive actions. At the very least such a force dropped behind the enemy positions would be likely to create confusion and interrupt communications and much needed supplies of food, ammunition and fuel to the dug-in German defenders along the Gothic Line.

The availability of a squadron of highly trained SAS paratroopers at this time of extreme threat to the Allied lines in Italy was an ideal opportunity to put theory into practice and test out Major Lett's bold proposal. The rugged countryside and tree-lined mountain slopes of mainland Northern Italy offered considerable operational advantages for a unit such as the Special Air Service. The SAS specialised in working in small groups of highly mobile, highly trained paratroopers, operating deep behind the enemy lines for optimum surprise and impact on the enemy communications, supplies and morale. They had been used elsewhere to great effect to prepare the way for wider offensives and as a means of tying up and diverting enemy forces away the front line.

However, Allied High Command decided that only 10 per

cent of the force requested by Major Lett would be sent. It was considered too dangerous to risk a larger force given the uncertainties of what they might find on the ground, coupled with the ever increasing list of competing priorities and demands for SAS forces elsewhere.

Consequently, the plan for SAS Operation Galia was conceived and put into practice in little over two weeks and consisted of just 33 officers, NCOs and other ranks.

Operation Galia began on the 27th December 1944.

Photo of sticks from the Galia Squadron taken in September 1945. Front row (left to right) Cpl. Larley, Sgt. 'Smokey' Lidington, Sgt. Chalky Wright, Capt. Bob Walker Brown (CO Galia), Sgt. Rookes, Sgt. Johnie Johnson (wireless operator), Cpl. Reg Everett. Middle row (left to right) Bill Whitaker, Don Hempstead, 'Spud' Taylor, Eric 'Lofty' Kennedy, Jimmy Church, me ('Spam'), Cpl. Ford. Back row (left to right) Pct. Tate, wireless operator Joe Cunningham, Sir John Matthews (we called him 'Sir John' because he spoke like a toff and used to frighten squaddies by shouting at them in a plumby officer's voice), Harry 'Jock' Shanley.

Chapter 2
The plan

It was a week or two before Christmas 1944. Number 3 Squadron 2nd SAS had been deployed behind the lines in France where we had operated alongside the Maquis, the French Resistance. After we had helped liberate the town of Langres we were pulled out and sent to Italy. We were told we'd be going to Rome, which had been liberated in May, for a bit of rest and relaxation. Sounded great. I'd never been abroad until I joined up and there's me, all set to celebrate Christmas in the Eternal City with the lads. Of course, it didn't turn out like that. The bloody Third Reich had other ideas.

We all thought Jerry was beat. The papers said the Allies were just waiting for winter to end before finishing the job. The first inkling that anything was wrong came when one of our lads listened (against orders of course) to 'Axis Sally', the German propaganda station on the wireless. She boasted that Germany had turned the war around in the Ardennes, where a major German offensive operation was underway. None of us believed it at first but the BBC later confirmed that eight panzer divisions had broken through on a 40-mile front, threatening the Allied gains near Antwerp. Hitler's last stand, they call it now, or the Battle of the Bulge. They had tanks, heavy guns and even Krauts with Yankie accents wearing stolen US Army uniforms to create confusion. Bloody impressive, given they had been on the run since D-Day.

There was pandemonium. A lot of our lads from the French, Belgian and 1 Squadron SAS were rushed in, along with the Yanks – the American Airborne 101st – paras like us – to fill the gaps and stop Jerry breaking through. Our lot, 2nd SAS, were lucky – or so we thought. We were too far away to get mixed up in that. What we didn't know was that intelligence reports from the Italian partisans indicated that Uncle Albert (Commander of the Axis Forces in Italy, Field Marshal Albert Kesselring), as we called him, was planning to launch a similar massive counter-attack in Italy.

In Italy, the Allies had fought their way up from the south since the
Eyeties gave up and came over to our side in September '43. Each time
our lads seemed on the brink of a break through, that wily old sod
Kesselring retreated with his troops and dug in. The last major
defensive position was the heavily fortified Gothic Line which
stretched the entire width of the country from east to west. The
Germans had dug in defensively in Northern Italy and since D-Day
the Allies had been stretched, fighting on two fronts. The prospect of
a major German attack on the Italian east coast, near Livorno, could,
it was feared, sever supply lines to the Allied armies. That prospect
set alarm bells ringing at Allied HQ.

The call came out for volunteers and, being young and stupid, we
stepped forward. Christmas was cancelled along with any thoughts of
'RnR' in Rome.

The plan was for a group of us to parachute in deep behind enemy
lines in the mountains. There, we were to link up with the local
partisans, split into 'sticks' (small groups) of five or six and then
launch attacks on the German's from the rear. Our job was to put the
fear of God into the enemy. Hit them hard. Create merry hell. Blow
up communication lines, ambush enemy troops and marching columns
heading for the front.

The drop was to take place in daylight so Jerry could see us coming.
With all our equipment, weapons and supplies, the hope was, from a
distance, we could fool them into thinking a whole parachute brigade
had landed behind them. That would divert them away from any
planned offensive and force them to chase after us instead. The Yanks
would then move into the positions left by the enemy as they chased
after us.

Simple.

Thirty odd blokes, including officers and NCOs, were selected from
those who volunteered. Me, Jimmy and Lofty Kennedy were chosen
along with Reg Everett and our Sergeant, Chalky Wright.

Reg Everett was a country boy who spoke with a broad Somerset
accent. Reg was able to slink into a hen house and come out with a
hat full of eggs without a single 'cluck' being heard. Just the sort of
specialist skill we needed on this trip. On survival training in Scotland
he demonstrated his finely honed foraging, fishing and poaching
skills. Unfortunately, the Scottish salmon industry took a while to
recover from the speed fishing technique Reg pioneered which
involved hand grenades.

Our Sergeant, Chalky Wright, had been in the police before joining up. He was solid and dependable in a crisis but a real practical joker the rest of the time.

Our commander, Captain Bob Walker Brown, was a tough, stocky Scot with a bristling moustache and boundless energy. He wasn't one for a laugh and a joke with the lads and with his double-barrelled surname and Scottish bur we weren't sure about him at first. However, it wasn't long before he had our respect. We found out about his war record for starters. Walker Brown had had an eventful war. In June 1942 he'd served with the Highland Light Infantry in North Africa but had been badly wounded, captured and shipped to Italy to kick his heels in the notorious Chieti POW camp. When the Italian armistice was announced in September 1943 he, along with other POWs, took the opportunity to escape before the German's took over guard duty from the Italians. He was, therefore, well acquainted with the terrain and conditions he was about to face in Northern Italy. Walker Brown had also led us on our last mission, behind the lines in France. If the Guv'nor ever said 'Well done Laddie!' you knew you'd earned it. He wouldn't ask us to do anything he wouldn't do himself. He was a born leader, hard as nails, tough as old boots and we'd have followed him to hell and back – as indeed, we did.

The operation was codenamed 'Galia'. I still don't know why they picked that name. None of us gave it much thought at the time. We had enough to keep us occupied. We weren't told exactly where we were going but they did tell us we would have to take as much with us as possible.

We had just a week to prepare and get all our equipment together and to make sure our weapons were up to scratch and in fine working order. We wrote letters home to family and friends which 'for security reasons' would only be despatched once the operation was underway.

The weather was terrible. Freezing cold even where we were in Bari on the Italian south-west coast. The whole of Europe was in the grip of the worst winter in living memory. In the mountains, where we were to be dropped, by all accounts it would be even worse. Blizzards, ice, snow, the lot. Given the conditions you would have thought they would make sure we had all the proper kit for winter warfare.

No chance.

We were dropped in what we stood up in. Ordinary uniforms, jump suits, khaki smocks, woolly jumpers and hobnail boots. Not exactly the ideal kit for an extended guerrilla campaign behind the lines, in

Arctic conditions.

The lack of adequate clothing and equipment, especially decent boots, was something that would come back to haunt us later – but there was a war on. There wasn't any point moaning about it. There were no shops or supermarkets or army surplus stores where we could pop out and stock up. So we begged, stole or borrowed whatever we could lay our hands on and made the best of it. As we would discover, the Germans were much better equipped. Skis, snow shoes, rubber-soled boots, camouflaged winter whites, waterproof anoraks, they had the lot. We couldn't help being envious of the way the Third Reich looked after their men in Italy.

Of course, it was a different story for the Germans on the Russian front.

We were supposed to go on Christmas Eve but for some reason we got stood down at the last minute. A few of us ended up celebrating Christmas, contrary to orders, in a bar in Bari. The small coastal town had only recently been liberated. There was still a danger of enemy spies and fascist sympathisers lurking in the shadows. During the evening a fight broke out in the bar, followed shortly afterwards by an explosion. The military police were quickly on the scene. Fifth columnists were suspected. We didn't want to stick around to help them with their inquiries. We made ourselves scarce and got back to barracks relatively unscathed, although one lanky member of our party was spotted with his uniform in tatters and cotton wool stuffed in his ears.

The day after Boxing Day, the whole squad was brought together at Brindisi Aerodrome for the final briefing and equipment check. Captain Walker Brown confirmed we were to operate in front of the US 5th Army behind enemy lines. We were to link up with local partisan bands and a SOE mission deep in the mountains at a drop zone, codenamed 'Huntsville'. The partisan force we were going to be operating with was known as the 'International Battalion' and it was commanded by a British Army Major called Gordon Lett. Our CO, Walker Brown, told us he knew Major Lett very well. They had both been POWs in the same camp in Italy. They had escaped, separately, after the Italians changed sides. Walker Brown had made it back to England where he joined our lot, but Major Lett had found shelter with the local mountain people and joined SOE as their man 'behind the lines'. So we had Major Lett to thank for cancelling our Christmas RnR in Rome. Operation Galia had been his idea. I made a mental note to 'thank' the Major if I got the chance.

We were given an estimate of the enemy's strength in the region. Nazi storm-troops (the SS) were said to have carried out reprisals against local civilians for partisan attacks. A specialist Mongolian Alpine regiment, experienced in mountain warfare, was active and likely to be deployed against us along with the Italian fascist forces known as the *Brigata Nera*.

The partisan situation wasn't clear cut either. There were reports of in-fighting among the many different partisan factions and particular difficulties with the communist bands. Convincing the communists to join forces to combat the common enemy had proved problematic in some areas. Their main incentive appeared to be to pilfer and hoard weaponry for a post-war revolution. Finally, we were warned to be on alert for spies and fascist sympathisers. Telling friend from foe, especially since most of us couldn't speak a word of Italian, was going to be a challenge.

The key objectives for attack included all major roads in the region. Intelligence suggested that most enemy troops moved at night to avoid attack from the air. Some food, equipment and supplies had already been dropped at the Huntsville drop zone but we were warned that food in the mountains was likely to be scarce and living conditions generally would be harsh.

The final briefing over, we lined up in front of our transport – a twin-engined DC 47 for a team photo. That done, we split up into our sticks and clambered aboard our allotted aircraft. Four Dakotas in all, accompanied by two Thunderbolt fighter planes.

The journey to Huntsville (Rossano) from Brindisi took around an hour. There was little banter between the lads due to the noise of the aircraft engines. Some of us had fags on the go to steady the nerves. I smoked 40 a day back then. They even partly paid us in Player's, Camel and Lucky Strike. If someone got injured or wounded the first thing we would do was stick a fag in their mouth. It probably wouldn't have made any difference had we known about the cancer link. We had more immediate dangers to face.

As we neared our destination, we got ready, clipped our static lines to the rail above our heads and waited anxiously for the green light to come on. Our Dakota, the lead aircraft, circled around the valley several times. The pilot was obviously having difficulty spotting the correct coded landing signals. Low cloud cover was a major problem given the geography and high mountain ranges surrounding the drop zone. We stood in line like that for what seemed like eternity.

Air pockets were a constant danger, dragging the aircraft suddenly down as we flew around the valley looking for the pre-agreed fires, lights and flags. At last the green signal came on for the first man to jump. This, it had been pre-determined, would be Lieutenant Chris Leng, a young SOE liason officer. He had volunteered to go first to make sure all was well. Using a Very flare gun, he was to send a signal for us to follow.

As Leng's chute unfolded, the old worries flooded back. Would our chutes open? Where would we land?

Twisted or sprained ankles were commonplace after parachute jumps but were not too much of a long-term concern. Fractures of any sort though would be disastrous on an operation like this.

Would we face a hostile reception as we came down? We'd be sitting ducks with no ability to fire back. All our weapons were stashed in leg bags, to be recovered, if we were lucky, on landing. Besides we needed both hands to steer and hold the parachute harness before landing. We had all learned the trick of snapping off the release and hanging onto the harness straps immediately before landing to prevent being dragged along by the wind.

Although he didn't tell us at the final briefing, Walker Brown had a good deal more to worry about than the drop. The adverse weather conditions had made radio communications impossible with SOE. A morse code message had arrived just prior to our briefing, purporting to come from Blundell Violet, the codename of the SOE operative on the ground at the drop zone. Experienced morse code operators could pick up the slightest variations in transmission patterns. An unusual transmission pattern had been detected that morning. It was possible the SOE mission had been captured, the operator transmitting under duress.

Despite this risk, the decision had been taken to proceed with the operation but to send a guineau pig in first as a precaution. Lieutenant Leng had volunteered for the honour. As it turned out, the signaller at Rossano had been suffering from frostbite but Walker Brown didn't know that as he scanned the ground anxiously for the 'all clear' signal.

At last the signal was spotted and the Captain launched himself from the doorway of the DC 47.

No-one could have foreseen the reception that awaited us on the ground.

A Whitley Bomber - better know to us as 'the flying coffin'. We dropped through a hole in the floor trying not to 'ring the bell' on the way out.

My stick before take off...I'm first in line far left

A shot of me shaking hands with stick commander Sgt. Chalky Wright and 'Johnie' Johnson shortly before Galia, with the Dakota in the background.

Gearing up for the Jump!

Left to right Johnnie Johnson (back view no hat), Harry (Jock) Shanley in foreground looking at the camera,
Pat Duggan at the rear, back view with hat and pack, Ted Robinson in foreground back view with hat and pack,
Lieutenant Shaughnessy looking left no hat. Me-extreme right adjusting girths

'Fixing chutes five minutes before take off'. I am the paratrooper in profile in the foreground. The third trooper in the photo is Ted Robinson. The second paratrooper is Lieut. Riccomini.

Chapter 3
Reception at Rossano

One by one, we followed the Captain and baled out, tumbling into the freezing void beyond. I felt a tug above me after a few seconds. Thankfully, the canopy opened. I floated down through the dark storm clouds as the biting, blustery wind battered me from every direction. We jumped at about 1,000 feet so I knew didn't have long to hang about up there. Every now and again I would catch a glimpse of other parachutes either side and below. The steep mountain slopes and valley floor were blanketed with snow which, with the low cloud cover, made it difficult to judge distance and distinguish earth from sky. Braziers had been lit to help guide us to the target drop zone. At one end of a field near a ruined village, a pair of huge British and Italian flags had been laid out flat on the ground so as to stand out against the snowy white backdrop. Tiny, ant-like figures scurried around the bundles which had already landed.

We had been at war with Italy only a year or so. The Allies were now busily bombing Italian cities and invading from the south. How these people would react to us dropping by to see in the New Year was anybody's guess, but I would soon find out. Mercifully, the blustery wind died down the closer I got to landing and I could hear the heartening sound of cheering from the villagers and partisans lining the edges of the drop zone.

The ground came rushing up to meet me. In one movement I pressed the harness release but held on tightly to the straps. I bent my knees to cushion the impact. The thud on landing knocked the breath from my body regardless.

Excited villagers cheering and crying 'Inglesi! Inglesi!' pulled me upright. Old ladies dressed in black kissed me on both cheeks. Half-starved kids with bright, shiny eyes skipped and danced around my feet. Several bearded, swarthy, fierce-looking partisans appeared. Some, rather disconcertingly, wore German uniforms or tunics with ammunition bandoliers criss-crossing their chests. The partisans insisted on embracing me – garlic-breath kisses on both cheeks, bear hugs and hefty pats on the back.

Meanwhile, men, equipment and supplies were landing all over the drop zone and beyond. We had a job keeping track of them and ensuring no-one was hit on the head by the heavy loads. In all the excitement this seemed to be the gravest danger we faced. Some chutes carrying equipment and supplies fell beyond the main landing field and drifted into a deep gorge where the river flowed into a nearby dam. Others got caught in olive groves or in the branches of the chestnut trees that clung to the slopes of the valley. The majority, though, landed on or near the target drop zone itself. A minor miracle, given the conditions.

After about half an hour the last of the 300 or so parachutes had been dispatched from the Dakotas. The partisans and locals eagerly helped us to collect the containers and equipment bags together so we could take stock of weapons, ammunition and other essentials. I spotted Jimmy Church, Kennedy and Reg Everett and made my way through the throng towards them. Even Kennedy had made it down unscathed. We quickly changed our helmets for the warmer, more comfortable SAS red berets.

'Like bloody Piccadilly Circus around 'ere 'ain't it,' remarked Jimmy looking around.

'Yea, all we need is the statue of Eros,' replied Reg.

We watched the lead Dakota complete its final sweep of the valley. Dipping its wings in a farewell salute, the formation disappeared into the clouds for the last time to head back to the relative safety of Brindisi aerodrome.

As the plane disappeared and the sound of the engines died away, there were a few grumbles about 'bloody Yanks, always getting the cushy jobs and toasting their tootsies by the fire in an hour', but it was just banter. We all understood we would be totally dependant on the skill and daring of the American pilots to re-supply us over the coming weeks and that they had done a pretty amazing job to get us here at all, given the conditions.

We retrieved as many bags of equipment as possible and gathered them together for temporary storage. We were ordered to parade and stood to attention while our Sergeant, Chalky Wright, called the roll. All were present and correct, except Lieutenant Riccomini, our only Italian speaker. The drop had been Ricky's first parachute jump and the decision to bring him along had been a calculated risk given his value to the operation. The Guv'nor was not best pleased to find his translator had gone AWOL just when he needed him most.

There were a few minor injuries. Parachutists Hildage, Mulvey and Shanley had the misfortune to land on the steep-sided, terraced vineyard situated to one side of the drop zone. One had turned his ankle, others had cuts and bruises but nothing too serious. After the roll call, one of the partisans, gaunt faced with stick thin arms, tanned walnut-brown and sporting a full beard, was invited by our CO to step forward. Two years living incognito amongst the locals meant Major Lett was virtually indistinguishable from the other partisans surrounding us.

'We are certainly glad to see you lads. You may have heard something of the partisans here. They are good chaps and are putting up a fine show, against tremendous odds. The village you see over there is what is left of Chiesa di Rossano. The Nazis burned it to the ground in reprisal for partisan actions. The nearest enemy garrison is at Pontremoli, which is about four hours march from here. There is no possibility of danger for at least forty-eight hours. After that it will be as well to be prepared. Now if you go over to that hut which you see among the trees you will find a very courageous old lady who has prepared a pot of tea for you.'

It didn't take long, despite the language barrier, for friendships to be forged between the locals and us. A lovely old lady, Mama Deluchi, wielded a ladle serving the tea, while other helpers added milk from a copper saucepan and distributed pieces of hot chestnut bread. We had never tasted chestnut bread before but I didn't hear anyone turn it down. We couldn't believe our luck. We were expecting to have to get ready to do battle almost as soon as we landed, given we were well behind enemy lines, but here we were being treated like visiting royalty and drinking cups of tea. Not that we were complaining.

A little later we were all taken into the village for supper. A relaxed party atmosphere took over as the wine started to flow. A great cheer went up when, finally, Lieutenant Riccomini, our translator, made his belated appearance. He had veered off course in the strong winds and had landed in a tree a few miles away. The startled villagers of neighbouring Peretola had helped him down. To add to his misfortune he'd cut his foot and was limping badly.

The old church clock in the ruined village of Chiesa di Rossano chimed midnight as the fiesta drew to a close. Jimmy, Kennedy, Reg and I had the good fortune to be billeted together in the cellar of the only inn.

The innkeeper was a ruddy-faced, jolly chap, called Salvatore. He must have been in his seventies and was as thin and as fit as a whippet. He insisted we joined him for a last bottle of grog before we got our heads down. As we were later to discover, Salvatore always had a ready supply of home-made wine somewhere about his person and was roaring drunk most of the time. Salvatore owned the few mules which were left in the area. It was impossible to move around the mountains in the conditions we faced without pack animals. The mules were Salvatore's pride and joy and he treated them like his babies. Salvatore also knew the mountains like the back of his hand, so his value as a guide would be highly prized in the days to come. We accepted his hospitality with good grace even though we were, by then, exhausted by the day's events. The conversation was a bit stilted since Salvatore couldn't speak much English and we were similarly hampered with Italian. We made do with the usual hand signals and speaking loudly. At one point Salvatore stood up, composed himself and solemnly proposed a toast.

'Victory', he slurred and, raising both hands in true statesman-like fashion, he then gave us a double 'V' sign. We fell about laughing, much to his confusion. We put him straight.

'That way's for Hitler, mate. This way's for Churchill!'

For days afterwards old Salvatore could be seen parading about practising double 'V' signs to Hitler and Churchill respectively.

We were woken early next morning by the rural chorus of cocks crowing, barking dogs and bird song. The 'one for the road' we had shared with our host had done its job and we'd all slept soundly despite the cold, hard floor penetrating the straw Salvatore had thoughtfully provided. For a brief moment, the peaceful sounds of the countryside made the war seem a very long way away.

We were soon brought back to reality.

The Captain divided us into six 'sticks' of five men plus an HQ stick. Leaders of each stick were selected from the officers and NCOs. Partisan volunteers supplemented each SAS stick to guide them to designated ambush points. Once in position our orders were to wait until suitable targets appeared, such as enemy troops, vehicles or marching columns. Some sticks had specific tasks such as blowing up particular roads or bridges. Generally our job was to carry out whatever harassment or disruption we could manage and to generally make a bloody nuisance of ourselves.

We'd met the young couriers of the local partisan band (known as the International Battalion) at the party the previous day. They were little more than boys really, aged between 17 and 20 at most. They were teamed up with their respective sticks and were already getting to know the men they would soon be leading through the mountains, trying, at the same time, to find ways to communicate in the absence of a common language.

One of the biggest problems we faced was contacting HQ in Bari. In those days radio or wireless communication was pretty rudimentary. Our radios only transmitted messages and only then if we were lucky. The bad weather, high winds, the steep mountain ranges and atmospherics all contributed to frustrate radio contact. We just had to hope for the best and trust that messages got through. Morse code was used but that too had its limitations.

Jimmy Church was in number five stick led by Lieutenant Shaughnessy, a tough, no-nonsense Irishman who had been with us on survival training in Scotland. Jimmy's stick were ordered to set off immediately and to head south in order to cross the river Magra. Their orders were to attack enemy columns using the road through the mountains from Modena. A young lad called Chella was picked as their guide from the valley of Valeriano. He knew the terrain Jimmy's stick were going to go through very well. Number five stick were the only unit sent south.

I was in number one stick led by Sergeant Wright. Reg Everett, Lofty Kennedy and Corporal Johnson, our radio operator, were with us. We were given two guides, Bruno Cura and Falco, who were to lead the way. We set off to our first objective, the village of Buzzo with orders to harrass the enemy columns in the Borgo Taro area. The weather, as we left our HQ at Rossano, had taken a turn for the worse. Snow and ice covered the mountain paths and a cold wind from the north swept up the slopes, piling up snow drifts across the mule tracks.

We hadn't got very far when a formation of American Dakotas flew very low over our heads towards the Rossano valley we had just left. Corporal Johnson swore under his breath. The message he'd sent earlier cancelling the drop which had been planned prior to our departure obviously hadn't got through. The planes flew on towards the Hunstsville drop zone but were soon obscured from view by the mountains. A few minutes later we heard a distant 'crump' followed shortly after by a plume of dark smoke rising over the nearest mountain range. We all knew it was bad news and decided to turn back to see if there was anything we could do.

The Dakota had been sucked down by an air pocket and had crashed into a wooded hillside near Rossano. The plane caught fire instantly and all seven aircrew aboard perished. Our first sombre task, before we'd even seen any sign of the Nazis, was to recover their bodies and bury the airmen in the little cemetery at the church of Chiesa di Rossano.

Our squad formed a guard of honour and representatives from all the partisan formations came to pay their respects. Losing a supply plane and its whole crew before we'd fired a shot in anger was a bad enough blow to our morale in these early days, but the ramifications of this loss were to have a more far-reaching impact on Operation Galia.

A supply drop at Rossano during Operation Galia.

SAS stick behind enemy lines. I am third from the right on the back row.

Chapter 4
One step forward, two steps back

The day after we buried the unfortunate aircrew was New Year's Eve. With the exception of Jimmy's stick, which had already headed south, the remainder of the squad, together with the partisan units, set off in the opposite direction for the village of Sero. This mountain-top outpost was to be the staging point for many of the raids we intended to carry out on the enemy communication lines and main roads in the area.

It was a difficult climb to the village, along the steep, slippery mountain tracks. In some places even the mules got stuck in the snow. We had to unload the equipment and carry it across the patches of ice and then load up the mules again before we could continue. It was time-consuming, energy-sapping work. One step forward, two steps back, but it was the only way to get heavy stores, equipment and ammunition from one place to another. Our army issue hob-nailed boots were useless and had no grip. We slipped about on the ice and sparks flew up when we scuffed the rocks and boulders underfoot, increasing the danger of discovery by enemy patrols. The Captain eventually had to dip into ops cash to pay a local cobbler to knock us up some proper footwear more suited to the conditions. We had no winter camouflage kit either and against the snowy backdrop our khaki jumpsuits made us stick out like cherries on a wedding cake.

Corporal Johnson sent a message to HQ asking for proper warm, 'white' clothing to be dropped, but all they sent us was a year's supply of PT vests. The desk-side Johnnies must have thought we needed the exercise.

We reached the hill-top village of Sero after a full day's slog. There we were met by one of the leaders of the local resistance movement, Louis 'Pippo' Siboldi. Pippo had served in the Italian navy and his brawny forearms were covered in tattoos. A big, bull of a man with a huge, black, bushy moustache, he spoke fluent English but with a strong New York, Brooklyn waterfront accent, peppered with expletives. Although he must have been in his early sixties, Pippo was very fit and, of course, knew his way around the Apennine mountains. Within minutes of meeting us he had got to know every member of the SAS squad by name. His infectious laughter and booming presence really lifted our spirits. He was to become invaluable to us over the forthcoming weeks as guide, translator and auxillary member of the SAS. Corporal Johnson installed the radio set in one of the bedrooms of Pippo's house, which became our battle HQ for the next nine weeks.

Pippo insisted on taking part in our first attack planned for that night. It was nearly midnight and, even though we'd hardly got our breath back from the climb to Sero, the Captain was determined to see the New Year in with an early morning 'fire-work display' at the town of Borghetto Di Vara. Borghetto was situated about ten miles north-west of La Spezia and had special significance as a target for us since it was the HQ of the fascist militia. Many German and Italian fascist troops were garrisoned there and we decided to launch the attack at daybreak. This was a calculated risk, designed to demonstrate to the enemy that we had sufficient personnel and daring to launch an offensive against such a well-defended position. We hoped it would put the fear of God into them so that they would call for re-enforcements from the front lines.

To carry the heavy weapons including the Vickers machine guns, mortars and ammunition, the mules were needed to transport the loads virtually to the firing point. The Captain asked for volunteers from the muleteers to assist us. Before any of the young lads could respond, our friend, the gregarious, elderly innkeeper, Salvatore, leaped forward. He wouldn't countenance any of his younger charges being selected for the 'honour' of leading the SAS into battle.

Dawn approached. As silently as we could, the mixed band of SAS, partisans and fully laden mules approached the spot chosen to launch the surprise attack. As we got near we noticed that instead of leading the mules, the mules were now leading Salvatore. Filled to the brim with wine, Salvatore was literally staggering along, clinging to his poor beast's tail. Nothing would persuade him to stay behind and sleep off the effects of the home-made hooch while the attack took place. We didn't have time to argue with him. We were just grateful that he hadn't started to sing.

Captain Walker Brown positioned us carefully to ensure maximum surprise and to give us a sporting chance to escape back into the mountains as soon as the attack was over.

Galia was the first SAS Operation to use 3″ mortars. The weapon had a maximum range of 2,700 yards and was normally fine for attacking a single target but wasn't very effective against scattered or separated targets. Its main drawback was that it weighed a ton. Also, only the Captain and Lofty Rose had been trained to fire them and only two of the parachutists on Galia (Sgt. Rookes and Corporal Larley) had been fully trained to operate the Vickers machine guns. Fortunately, we were quick learners.

Having carted them all this way, we were determined to make best use of the mortars in this first attack on the enemy garrison at Borghetto. On the signal from our CO, we launched a fearsome barrage from 1,000 yards. Over 30 mortar bombs rained down on houses previously identified from partisan intelligence reports to be occupied by German and Italian fascist units. There were direct hits on a number of the targets. Complete surprise was achieved. Our Bren gunners followed up the mortar attack, focusing on two enemy lorries and a car which had the misfortune to be driving through the town. The partisans joined in the attack taking up firing positions to the South of Borghetto, preventing the enemy from escaping into the mountains.

The attack was soon over and the Captain gave the order to withdraw. Salvatore, still in an alcoholic daze, once again grabbed hold of his unfortunate mule's tail which proceeded to pull both him and its heavy load up the hill again to the comparative safety of Sero. This time he did burst into song and there was nothing we could do to shut him up, his full baritone resounding over the hills as we made our escape. In the days to come, Salvatore described to all and sundry how he and his compatriot Pippo Siboldi had taken part in the wonderful *festa* at Borghetto. Both Pippo and Salvatore became permanent members of SAS raiding parties after that and accompanied us everywhere, with Salvatore allowing his faithful mule to take over for the journey home when he reached a state of happy abandon.

Confirmation that we had made our presence felt came the following day. As we hoped would happen, panic and alarm spread among the German Army units and fascist militia stationed at Borghetto. Intelligence reported that following our attack the entire enemy garrison had withdrawn, fearful of further attacks. They returned, with re-enforcements, some 24 hours later – just in time to be greeted by a further SAS offensive on the town. The main roads in the area provided the only means by which enemy convoys could move by land from Genoa to La Spezia. The enemy also needed these roads to re-supply their front-line forces along the Gothic Line. Our job was to try to prevent them launching an offensive and to turn around and chase us instead. Lieutenant Riccomini's stick (Pcts Gargan, Shanley, Sumptor and Hildage) mined a road bridge which crossed a river on the 4th January near the village of Valeriano. The mine was detonated as an enemy truck crossed the bridge. Reports confirmed over 20 enemy troops had been killed or wounded.

Attacks and ambushes on these roads by the combined SAS sticks and partisan units were carried out in quick succession to keep the pressure on. A few days later it was my turn. Our stick, led by Sergeant Chalky Wright, reached our allotted ambush point on the Spezia to Genoa road an hour before dawn. We laid flat in the snow on our bellies on either side of the road, weapons at the ready, waiting for a suitable target to appear. We shivered uncontrollably, fingers and toes numbed with cold. Eventually, we heard the laboured throb of a car engine coming up the hill towards us. The adrenaline kicked in and the freezing conditions were forgotten as the vehicle came into view. A staff car, swastika pennant flying from the bonnet.

Chalky Wright gave the signal to open fire.

Caught between two withering bursts of automatic fire from either side, the four occupants, taken by surprise, had no opportunity to shoot back. Three of them somehow managed to scramble out and, although wounded, using darkness as cover, escaped into the surrounding countryside. The fourth lay slumped in a bloodied heap on the front passenger seat. The partisans quickly confirmed the dead man's identity, a high-ranking fascist official. A briefcase chained to his wrist contained a substantial amount of cash; in excess of 125 million lire duly 'liberated' for the partisan cause.

Our stick, with Pippo and his men, marched back into Sero in high spirits. The attacks had gone well despite the weather, the hardships and the set backs. We felt we were beginning to make an impression. We were helping the locals to fight back against the Nazi and fascist oppressors. We could feel the morale and spirits of the local partisans and civilians begin to lift as a result.

Later, back at Sero, number two stick (led by Lieut. Riccomini) and the Captain's HQ stick, were present as we stood in line side by side with the partisans and were debriefed about our exploits and those of our comrades by the Captain (speaking to us) and Major Lett (addressing the partisans in Italian). The Captain began by commending us on our work so far. Walker Brown was a tough old stick and he didn't give praise lightly so we were feeling pretty good about ourselves at that point.

Nothing prepared us for the body blow to come.

Earlier that day Major Lett had received a message sent by the neighbouring partisan commander Lieut. Dani Buchioni. Number 5 stick, the only SAS stick sent south to attack the area around Aulla and Reggio, and their Italian guide had been captured by the *Brigata Nera* (fascist militia) near a mountain village called Montebello. In a grave, steady voice the Captain gave it to us straight.

Lieut. Shaughnessy, Sgt. Harrold, Cpl. Benson, Pct. Phillips, Pct. Mitchell and, of course, my pal, Pct. Jimmy Church were all 'in the bag'. The young partisan guide called Leonardo Chella had been leading them through the mountain passes. Apparently, a spy had tipped off the *Brigata Nera* about the presence of British paratroops in the area. Chella had been shot as a warning to the Montebello villagers against collaboration with the British. The SAS men had been taken away in trucks to an unknown destination.

The Major tried his best to soften the blow and promised to try to get any information about their whereabouts from partisan intelligence contacts in La Spezia. We knew, however, that the chances of Jimmy, Lieut. Shaughnessy and the others surviving were slim. We had heard stories of how the enemy treated SAS men captured behind the lines. We didn't need it spelling out.

Pippo, Salvatore and the other partisans became very emotional when they heard about Chella's execution. It was a bitter blow, especially after the euphoria of our own successful shoots but we could do nothing for our captured comrades.

Despite the Major's best efforts, we were to hear nothing further as to the fate of our friends during the remainder of the Galia operation.

To add to our sombre mood, the Captain told us that the US Airforce had refused, point blank, to drop any more supplies at the Huntsville drop zone believing it to be too dangerous following the loss of one of its aircraft and crew. Instead, an alternative drop zone (codenamed 'Halifax') was selected.

Whilst this decision may have made sense to the desk-bound

planners looking at their maps in Bari, from our perspective it was clear the decision had been made without regard to the conditions we faced on the ground. For starters, the new drop zone Halifax was a considerable distance from our Rossano or Sero HQs. It would take us five hours or more to trek through mountainous terrain in the snow and ice just to get there, running the risk of meeting enemy patrols along the way. We then had the problem of moving the supplies to a safe storage site. This would be no easy task in the atrocious weather conditions, with enemy troops surrounding the area and with communist bands of partisans prowling around interested in stealing supplies for their own purposes. We were completely reliant on air-dropped supplies of ammunition, food and other essential equipment to continue guerrilla operations. No amount of persuasion would budge the Americans, however, and from this point on we faced huge logistical re-supply difficulties which we somehow had to overcome. Much of our time and energy was wasted tracking down, collecting, transporting and guarding the stores.

Our worst fears about the communist partisans were soon realised just a week later. The communist Justice and Liberty Partisan Brigade from Pieve fired on us during a supply drop and later attempted to loot food and cigarettes from the supplies. Captain Walker Brown fired his pistol in the air. The communists ran a couple of hundred yards before turning and firing back at us. We replied with two Bren magazines above their heads and a third into their midst and they escaped with no casualties. Complaints were duly sent to the Italian partisan commander. He was a good, capable officer called Colonel Fontana, who commanded the respect of the resistance groups operating in the area, regardless of their politics. The harassment from the communists largely stopped as a result but the damage had been done as far as we were concerned. We avoided operating with the communist partisans after that because we felt we couldn't trust them.

The dangers for us and the Italian civilians and our comrades-in-arms, were ever present and likely to increase as we continued to tweak the Nazi tiger's tail. Partisan intelligence reports suggested that local enemy commanders, exasperated by the growing resistance, were planning a crackdown to flush out the partisans and parachutists operating in the 4th Operative Partisan Zone – the area we were operating in.

By the 11th January, despite the pilfering by the communists, we had enough supplies to recommence offensive operations. A recce party consisting of Walker Brown, Lofty Rose, Jock Shanley and Pct. Sumptor checked out the potential for a further attack on Borghetto. The recce showed that the road bridge over the river L'Ago would be an ideal spot for an attack. The new fascist HQ had also been identified. Whilst our stick returned to the Halifax drop zone to prepare for another drop, Lieutenant Riccomini and his men ambushed the bridge, while the remainder of the squad took up position 300 feet from the fascist HQ building in Borghetto Di Varo and make ready to attack. Ricky told me what happened later.

As the SAS got into position two fascist soldiers started an impromptu game of tennis in the road, unaware of the imminent danger they were in. Just as the attack was about to start, a column of vehicles could be heard coming into the town square towards the smaller of the two ambush parties. Since this group had only one Bren gun they decided to wait until the vehicles had passed to enable the larger party, which had five Bren guns, to attack the vehicles further up the road. With no radio communications this was a risky strategy but fortunately both the SAS sections were on the same wave-length. The main ambush party began the attack and peppered the German trucks and vehicles with Bren-gun fire. The recce party joined in and opened fire from the rear. The vehicle column, which included a captured British staff car, a ten-ton lorry full of equipment and several transporters carrying troops bound for the front, found itself suddenly the centre of a murderous cross-fire. The lorry, captured staff car and trucks were all destroyed by incendiary rounds fired by the main SAS squad. A substantial number of enemy soldiers were killed or wounded (around 26 according to later reports). The surviving enemy soldiers, in disarray, not knowing how many enemy they were facing or even in which direction to fire, ran in all directions seeking whatever cover they could find. In the confusion and panic, the SAS parties swiftly and quietly withdrew.

The following day reprisals began in earnest.

Hitler's Commando Order[1]

From 1942 onwards, when the tide of the war began to turn against him, Hitler ordered the extermination of captured Allied commandos. Captured soviet partisans were summarily shot as a matter of course. The Fuhrer's 'Top Secret Commando Order' of the 18th October 1942 was found among Nazi documents after the war. It stated:

> From now on all enemies on so-called commando missions in Europe or Africa challenged by German troops, even if they are in uniform, whether armed or unarmed, in battle or in flight, are to be slaughtered to the last man.

In a supplementary directive issued the same day Hitler explained to his commanders that the reason for his order was due to the success of the Allied commandos:

> I have been compelled to issue strict orders for the destruction of enemy sabotage troops and to declare non compliance with these orders severely punishable . . . It must be made clear to the enemy that all sabotage troops will be exterminated without exception to the last man. This means their chances of escaping with their lives is nil . . . Under no circumstances can they expect to be treated according to the rules of the Geneva Convention . . . If it should be necessary to initially spare one man or two, then they are to be shot immediately after interrogation.

This particular order was to be kept a strict secret and commanders were ordered to destroy it after they had taken due note of its contents. It must have remained imprinted on their minds as there are many instances where they carried out the instructions to the letter.

For example, on the night of 22nd March 1944 two officers and 13 men of the 267th Special Reconnaissance Battalian of the US Army were landed by naval craft far behind German lines with orders to demolish a railroad between La Spezia and Genoa. All were in uniform and carried no civilian clothes. Captured two days later they were executed by firing squad without trial on the orders of General Anton Dostler, commander of the LXXVth German Army Corps.

Dostler was tried by a US tribunal after the war and contended he was merely following Hitler's Commando Order. He said he would have been court martialled himself had he not complied. This didn't wash with the tribunal. He was condemned to death in Rome on October 12th 1945.

---

1 Taken from *The Rise and Fall of the Third Reich* by William Shirer, 1990, Book Club Associates.

One of my shots of a stick of SAS paratroopers and partisan guides traversing a snow covered mountain trail with a mule to carry supplies and weaponry during the operation.

An SAS stick posing with the Vickers machine gun we used to such devastating effect.

SAS stick I'm second from left at the back

Chapter 5
Close encounters

We passed through a little town called Brugnato en route to the
Borghetto ambush the previous day. After the attack, the *Brigata Nera*
took their frustrations out on Borghetto's unfortunate neighbours the
very next day. The Captain watched the unfolding scene through his
field glasses and got more and more agitated. Houses were being
ransacked and set alight by the marauding Black Shirts and fascist
militia. The townsfolk were screaming, running in all directions, trying
to flee from the shooting and violence perpetrated by their countrymen.
After a few minutes the Captain decided enough was enough. Taking
the 3″ mortar and Bren guns with us we set off determined to give them
a taste of their own medicine.

A couple of hours later we were in position ready to launch our
follow-up attack. We used the mortar to attack the road bridge which
linked the two towns. Just as the Captain was about to give the order
we had a stroke of luck. Screaming down from the skies, a US
Thunderbolt fighter dive-bombed the town. It looked impressive even
though the bomb it dropped didn't explode. We followed up with a
mortar attack, firing three mortar bombs into the main road leading out
of Brugnato. The black shirts retreated towards the bridge over the
river, blundering straight into our ambush.

A 'battle royal' ensued.

The enemy, of platoon strength, returned fire from the southern side
of the bridge, so we lobbed mortars onto their positions. After a terrific
pounding, several of the fascist forces ran for the hills. We fired at
anyone attempting to ford the river.

The enemy changed tack and trundled up a large field gun which
had been sited in the centre of Borghetto. The big gun opened up on
us and could have done serious harm. Fortunately, we managed to score

a bulls-eye with the mortars, destroying the gun and killing the crew. The Captain hid the mortar launch point from enemy observation behind a hill which enabled us to continue the attack. Our SAS Bren gunners accompanied by partisans armed with Italian 'Breda' machine guns crawled forward to a position on the enemy's flank and from there, fired tracer bullets at the town, which set more buildings alight.

At around 4.00 pm, with ammunition running low, Walker Brown gave the order to end the attack and withdraw. Just as he did so we got another stroke of luck. This time a formation of four Thunderbolt fighters arrived on the scene and dive-bombed the bridge and strafed the road where the enemy were still putting up a fight. This caused even more confusion and panic. They must have been convinced that we, somehow, had the capacity to call in air fighter support.

If only!

As a last resort, the beleaguered fascist forces in Borghetto hurriedly transported an even bigger 105 mm field gun and shelled the mountain-side in our general direction. They had no real idea of our exact location. We managed to slip away unscathed over the mountains, back to our hideout HQ at Sero while they wasted valuable shells blowing craters in the abandoned hill-side.

We felt there was a good possibility that the attack by the US Thunderbolt fighter planes, coupled with the prolonged daylight offensive on Borghetto by the joint SAS/partisan forces, would convince the enemy that they faced a large, well-armed force of paratroopers in the mountains and that they really needed to do something about it or else suffer more attacks. Our deception operation seemed to be working.

Of course, whilst we had achieved our objectives in part, this also meant our small force was about to reap the consequences. We hoped our American allies would take advantage of the diversion we had created to launch a major attack on the Gothic Line. If not, we knew we would soon have to face the full wrath of an enemy hell bent on rooting out the 'terrorists' in their midst.

By mid-January there were signs that the Germans were indeed preparing to launch attacks on the 4th Partisan Zone on a much larger scale than ever before. Intelligence reports from La Spezia and other local sources, backed up by wireless reports received from the SAS HQ at Bari, indicated that the Germans had called in re-enforcements in the form of specially trained Mongolian ski troops. These troops were particularly unscrupulous and were feared and loathed in equal measure by the locals.

The weather had not improved and all the mountain passes in or out of the valley were ice-covered and blocked by deep snow drifts. On the bright side, the conditions also gave us a degree of protection and helped the *Rossanesi* to maintain a ready supply of mules and donkeys to move our stores, supplies and ammunition.

The partisan commander for the area, Colonel Fontana, called a council of war, summoning all the partisan leaders, Major Lett and Captain Walker Brown. The officers decided that attack was the best form of defence. A plan was drawn up under which combined partisan and SAS formations would strike the enemy in several different places, before the main Allied offensive on the Gothic Line began. Battle positions were allocated to the various partisan and SAS formations and co-ordinated attacks were planned to take place on the 18th and 19th of January.

Then we learned that Mussolini might be coming to pay us a visit. Intelligence reported Il Duce was expected to visit Pontremoli with a strong escort of German troops en route to inspect the Monte Rosa Division, a composite German/Italian Alpine formation who were defending the Gothic Line. This was too good to miss. An attack on Pontremoli to 'welcome' the fascist dictator was included in the battle plan.

One big problem we had by this stage was the fact that we were really beginning to feel the pace. The squad's fighting strength had been severely affected by sickness and injury. The freezing weather conditions and the constant physical pounding our bodies were taking due to the terrain were wearing us down. The consequences of being ill-equipped for winter warfare were now coming home to roost. In contrast, we faced battle-hardened enemy troops, some of whom were from specialist Alpine formations, trained and equipped for battle for the environment with white camouflage snow suits. Some even had skis and snow shoes.

We suffered a variety of ailments from the harsh, cold conditions, lack of food and the physical exertion which was, by this time, part of our day-to-day existence. We all had cuts, chapped lips, cracked knuckles and blisters which refused to heal in the cold weather, often turning septic. Among the more serious casualties was Lieutenant Riccomini who still hadn't recovered from the injuries he'd received when he landed in a tree after parachuting into Rossano. His injured foot became infected. Others in the team were suffering colds, fevers or had the beginnings of flu. Kennedy, in particular, was in a bad way with a hacking cough and flu-like symptoms we suspected might be the beginnings of pneumonia. Others had contracted dysentery or scabies, the result of a poor diet lacking nutrition, particularly fruit and vegetables, none of which were available in the mountains during winter.

Those SAS still able to carry on the fight were to be supplemented by a detachment of twenty partisans of the Centro Croce brigade. Their commander, 'Richetto' had sent his best lieutenant, a young lad called Nino Siligato, to lead the partisan squad into battle. Nino's group had travelled for two days over the mountains to join up with us. When he arrived, he athletically vaulted from the saddle of his pony and embraced his friend, Major Lett. Nino was a sailor from Southern Italy who had already helped many fugitive ex-prisoners and downed Allied airmen to escape to the Allied lines. His courage had earned him a hero's reputation among his people. Nino had vowed never to shave or cut his hair until his homeland had been liberated from the Nazis and fascists. His dark hair hung loosely around his shoulders. A bushy black beard and moustache completed his fearsome, charismatic, swash-buckling appearance. Nino spoke English but had a peculiar way of referring to himself in the third person. Bowing theatrically, his first words to us were;

'Here is Nino. He is ready to fight with you.'

On the afternoon of the 18th January, most of our SAS troop (with the exception of Lofty Rose, Kennedy, Riccomini, Gargan and Hildage who were all too ill to travel) along with the partisans of the International Battalion and the fully laden mules, set off for the hill-top village of Arzelato. This village, to us, had great strategic importance due to the high church tower from which the whole of the city of Pontremoli, and a considerable part of the Magra valley – all the way in the distance to the town of Villafranca – could be easily observed. From the church tower, the countryside fell away in steep, wooded slopes down to the outskirts of Pontremoli. It was a mystery as to why the Germans hadn't thought to destroy the tower since it was such an obvious observation point, but we weren't complaining.

Taking advantage of a bright interval in the weather just before sunset the officers identified the key targets in the city below, including the fascist barracks and HQ. At the northern end of Pontremoli was an old castle which had once been the stronghold of the Visconti family and later a fortress for the Emperor Charles V. It commanded the road originally built by Napoleon to the Cisa Pass, where many German convoys had already come to grief, courtesy of the partisans. We watched for enemy movement but all seemed strangely calm with no traffic of any kind on the city roads. The railway station stood out clearly even though it had been bombed and abandoned. From the church tower, Walker Brown selected an ambush position south of the town where a fast flowing river was situated between the road and the ambush position.

Some hours later, Major Lett and Captain Walker Brown briefed us all on the battle plan. The Captain and a contingent of SAS were to be accompanied by Nino and his partisans. We were to stage an ambush on the main road leading to the town of Villafranca. The fall-back plan in case of enemy interference was for the force to return to Arzelato and then to return to the Rossano valley by the same route we had travelled earlier that morning. If Rossano too had become occupied by the enemy, we were to make for Sero. In view of the difficulty of communication (there being no two-way radio available), once the ambush had started, there would be no means of communicating with the assault troops to warn them as to any developments at their rear. Major Lett, therefore, had to remain behind at Arzelato and judge the situation from the sounds of battle and the information he would obtain from messengers.

Meanwhile, the fascist troops had been sent re-enforcements. We estimated their strength at between 800 and 1,800 men. No convoys had reached Pontremoli by day because of the fear of air attack by USAAF fighters or partisans. Most of the vehicles and supplies were moved by night. We therefore planned to attack the roads and supply lines under cover of darkness. We thought we would have a reasonable chance of success as long as the enemy had not been tipped off in advance.

It was late afternoon. As darkness was falling our stick and the rest of the SAS contingent under Walker Brown's command gathered on the road to move off to the chosen ambush point. Corporal Johnson, our wireless operator, and the sick and injured SAS men, remained behind at Arzelato with Major Lett to co-ordinate the force's next move once the enemy had been 'stirred up' after the planned road attack took place outside Pontremoli.

As the SAS and partisan force marched past him, Nino approached the Major.

'Goodbye *Maggiore*. If Nino should not return, he wants you to have his horse. *Buona Fortuna!*' The two men shook hands and Nino hurried away after his men.

At around 7.00 pm, taking advantage of the pitch black of night, we got into position to attack the main road leading into Pontremoli. Only two heavy Vickers machine guns were unloaded to be used in the attack, both of which were sited so as to fire on fixed lines at a point where the road dropped around 50 feet on one side and a fast flowing river ran by on the other. We waited patiently for several hours. Then, as dawn began to break we saw a long column of vehicles approaching from Pontremoli. At the same time, a battery of horse-drawn field artillery also moved towards the town from the opposite direction. Just as the two columns met, the Captain gave the order to attack. We opened up with the two heavy Vickers machine guns at a range of about 300 yards.

It was pandemonium! Vehicles caught fire, horses bolted, still chained to the artillery pieces they were pulling. Men jumped into the river to escape the tracer bullets that were raining down on them, only to come under small arms fire from the partisan forces on the flanks. The damage inflicted by the Vickers machine guns to the horses was gruesome. Some of the poor beasts were eviscerated, innards cascading across the road.

Sadly, we could see no sign of any car pompous enough to be carrying Mussolini but that hardly mattered. We'd achieved our objective, caused mayhem and inflicted substantial casualties right in the heart of the enemy HQ.

But it nearly all went horribly wrong for us. At the height of the action, Walker Brown, looking through his binoculars, suddenly noticed a movement further down the road on our side. A column of ski troops, wearing dirty snow smocks and carrying their skis over their shoulders, was moving swiftly towards us and was less than 1,000 yards away. Had their snow smocks been clean the Guv'nor would never have seen them until it was too late. Had they used their skis they would have caught us easily, but Lady Luck smiled on us again.

We pulled out at the double. We had no option but to use the track we had approached by in the interests of speed even though this too had its dangers. On reaching the track leading to the mountains we discovered we were following another German column only about 200 yards in front of us.

We were, literally, the meat in the sandwich between two different enemy patrols.

With time and options running out, Walker Brown led us via a more direct route. We ploughed straight up through the waist-deep virgin snow at the side of the track, heading towards the deserted village of Noce, the gaunt ruins of which bore silent testament to previous Nazi reprisals. We had left the mules, the radio and supplies at this village and now the race was on to get there before the Germans.

The climb up the sheer mountain-side through deep snow was exhausting. The snow was so deep in places that we had to keep changing the lead man every ten minutes or so to plough our way through the drifts. We managed it somehow and were glad to find no sign of the enemy on arrival. Walker Brown kept the lookout and ordered us to rest. About ten minutes later he spotted two companies of enemy troops, spread out and advancing towards us, only about 1,000 yards away and 500 feet below our position.

We quickly decided the best chance of evading capture was to split up into smaller groups, and head for the village of Coroletta, which lay some ten miles across the rugged mountains. To travel as lightly and as quickly as possible we had to smash the radio, bury and destroy the codes in the deep snow. We also had to abandon the mules, the heavy weapons and ammunition, having first disabled the weapons by throwing the essential firing parts away. We did this as fast as we could but as we moved off we came under heavy mortar and small arms fire from the rapidly advancing German forces.

Greatly outnumbered, we withdrew and set off towards Coroletta. We made it as far as a village called Codolo, half-way to our destination. After a brief rest Nino and his partisans covered our backs, as we made our way on the last part of the journey to Coroletta. Soon after our departure Nino's band came under heavy attack from all sides. Before they could follow us they were encircled by the enemy. Greatly out-numbered, Nino and his men bravely stood their ground but after a fierce fire-fight, our partisan comrades, running short of ammunition, were captured.

We discovered later that six partisans, including Nino Siligato, the Major's great friend and charismatic local hero, had been summarily executed.

The enemy flooded the area and seemed to be everywhere. Walker Brown led us west towards the village of Rio where we again came under mortar fire. We had to leave Lieut. Riccomini, Pct. Sumptor and an injured Italian guide behind, hidden in a cave deep in the mountains near Torano, to follow on later the best they could when the *rastrellamento* had run its course.

The rest of us reached the village of Rio at 1700 hrs but half an hour later we were spotted and fired upon by a German artillery battery. So once again we were on our travels and this time headed north, towards the daunting peak of Monte Gottero.

By this time we were all exhausted, very cold, hungry and thirsty after all the tramping about we had done. All I really wanted to do was curl up and get some rest but the Captain asked for a couple of volunteers to make a recce to find the safest route back to Major Lett at Arzelato. Reg Everett piped up and said he felt pretty confident about finding his way back. I couldn't let Reg go off on his own so I volunteered to go with him.

By keeping off the tracks and hiding when we spotted enemy patrols, Reg and I managed to dodge the troops who were, by now, marauding through the towns and villages in force. We cursed our heavy, noisy, good-for-nothing boots because of the racket they made on the stony, slippery surfaces. At one point, a mile or two outside of Arzelato, as we were crossing a field, we heard voices speaking a language we didn't recognise. From the language we decided we had at last stumbled across the Mongolian mountain troops the locals feared so much. We dived down flat in the snow and crawled towards a large compost heap which had been piled up in a corner of the field. We quickly buried ourselves under the heap of old cabbages and rotting vegetation. We were just in time. From our foul smelling hidey-hole we silently watched as the boots of a column of enemy troops passed right by our heads.

It was clear Arzelato had been occupied by the enemy. The contingency plan in the event of attack, was for the Major and the others to move to Rossano and if that was occupied, to go from there to battle HQ at Sero. When the coast was clear Reg and I wearily set off again, keeping to the edge of the steep mountain trails to more easily evade any enemy patrols. We climbed solidly upwards for about four hours. Night had fallen and the wind was bitterly cold. We hadn't eaten anything substantial for about three days and we were on our last legs. We didn't know whether Major Lett, Kennedy and the others had escaped, nor whether the Rossano valley would be free of enemy troops. As we made our way cautiously into the valley, the moon came out from behind the clouds to light the way. As it did so a voice shouted something aggressively at us in Italian from behind.

We had no time to react. Reg and I stood stock still and slowly raised our hands above our heads.

Major Lett's account of the enemy attack on Arzelato and Sero[1]

Following the departure of Captain Walker Brown and the main SAS squad with Nino Sigilato and his men, I waited anxiously for events to take their turn. Reports began to filter through that the enemy had taken up position to block the route to the village of Codolo. Corporal Johnson and my courier Nello had been leading the supply train of mules to the village to meet up with the SAS force following their ambush on the Pontremoli road. Half-way to the village, just as the firing signalled the beginning of the SAS ambush on the Pontremoli road, they spotted a German patrol and had no option but to make their way back to Arzelato.

The enemy were on full alert and were making their presence felt. Arzelato is built on the side of a hill. I decided to move the sick paratroopers Rose, Gargan, Kennedy and Hildage and the other men under my command to a house at the highest point of the village, to enable us to slip away into the mountains if we were forced to make an emergency exit. It was a good decision. Rifle shots rang out from below almost as soon as we reached the house.

From our vantage point I could see the good citizens of Arzelato running for their lives towards the wooded mountain slopes and the enemy troops were spread out and streaming into the village, firing as they approached. Corporal Johnson quickly hid the wireless set and we loaded the spare mortar and ammo onto the mules. I led my group of partisans and sick SAS men into the mountains. To gain the shelter of the trees, we first had to cross a snow-covered mountain slope. To make matters

---

1   This account is an edited description of events as described in Major Lett's excellent account of his exploits behind enemy lines as an SOE officer and which includes chapters describing Operation Galia – see *Rossano: An Adventure of the Italian Resistance*.

worse, the mule pulling Salvatore overbalanced and nothing would induce the old innkeeper to leave it. We had to unload the mule to get it back on its feet. Then, with Salvatore hanging onto his faithful mules' tail, our rag-tag column was able to set off again.

As we crossed the open slope, a machine gun opened up on us from the base of the Arzelato church tower, our observation post of the previous day. We should have been an easy target against the white, snow covered slopes and were well within firing range. Fortunately for us, the initial burst of tracer bullets flew harmlessly over our heads. We struggled through the snow to reach the cover of the trees and I really didn't think we would make it as the gunner had plenty of time to adjust his sights. However, the gun fell silent and we reached the cover of the trees without taking casualties.

I later discovered what had happened.

Two of my partisan sentries guarding the village below heard voices on the road shortly before sunrise. They waited until three figures came into view and challenged them for the password. The three men turned out to be the advance guard of an enemy patrol. The partisans opened fire on them. At that moment, a machine gun opened fire from the church, behind the partisans. Realising they were surrounded by enemy troops, my men made good their escape. When it grew light a short time later, the machine gunner at the church spotted our column struggling through the snow on the slope ahead and opened fire. By a stroke of incredible good fortune, just at that moment, the German officer commanding the unit saw one of his men spreadeagled across the road on the edge of the village. He called off the gunners and got them to help him retrieve the body and strap it to a mule to be sent back to their base.

Thus the partisans of Arzelato saved their comrades from Rossano.

Sadly, I also discovered later that it was around this time in the nearby village of Codolo that my good friend Nino Siligato and six of his comrades had been captured and were summarily executed by an enemy patrol. Nino was a great friend and brave patriot. His loss was a savage blow to me and his compatriots alike but we didn't have much time to mourn his loss.

In similar fashion to Captain Walker Brown's party, a deadly game of cat and mouse ensued between the pursuing enemy forces and our group.

When we reached the Rossano valley we found the enemy were already approaching it from all sides. Despite their various ailments, the men of the SAS squad were fit enough to walk. Lofty Rose insisted on carrying the mortar, assisted by another parachutist named Gargan. Gargan's youthful looks had led to him being christened 'the Boy Bandit' by the locals.

There were only 30 rounds of ammunition left for the mortar and we had some doubt as to whether it was in full working order, but Lofty regarded the mortar much as Salvatore regarded his mules – they were indispensable and simply could not be left behind.

Clearly, with the enemy now all around, we couldn't stay at Rossano. So we set off again for the two-hour march across country through the snow drifts towards Monte Gottero, the highest mountain in the area. The weather had changed again for the worse. Heavy clouds covered the leaden sky and cold blasts of wind swept the snow into swirling eddies of white powder. Eventually, we reached the edge of the plateau where so many supply drops had been made in the previous few weeks. Through field glasses I could see enemy patrols marching along the road, through Chiesa, a village which had already been destroyed in an earlier

The enemy troops offered a provoking target for the SAS squad but because the enemy hadn't yet begun to burn the other villages in the Rossano valley we decided not to give them cause to start doing so. In any event, firing the mortar would have given away our position and we didn't have enough ammo for a pitched battle if they called in re-enforcements. Overall there was much to be lost and not a lot to gain from launching an attack. Instead, we reluctantly buried the mortar in the snow to assist our progress.

In the middle of the afternoon, we were greatly cheered by the sudden appearance of Pippo Sibaldi. He had managed to dodge the german patrols and had come from Sero to find us. His lively presence soon improved our morale even though he brought news that the enemy had already reached his village but had had to fight for its occupation. Pippo became our guide once again and as dusk descended we decided to head for what I hoped would be a partisan stronghold along the slopes and summit of Monte Gottero. I knew that partisans from the Centro Croce brigade would try to hold out against the enemy onslaught.

I sent out couriers Nello and Riboncia ahead to check the route. They hadn't returned by nightfall and so we had no choice but to set off and take a chance. Armed with two light machine guns and as much ammunition as we could carry, our small band of paratroopers and partisans set off north towards Monte Gottero. We didn't know it then but Walker Brown and his men had also chosen the same route for their escape.

By the time we reached the mountain's slopes it was clear all was lost. The various partisan forces had dispersed when the enemy had attacked in force. After much reflection, Pippo and I decided to retrace our steps and return to the Rossano valley. We reasoned that we had a better chance of survival and avoiding capture by navigating the towns and villages Pippo and I knew so well. We picked up other stragglers on the way including paratroopers sent by Captain Walker Brown from his squad to recce the route back to us.

*Partisan guide in battledress
leading a mule laden with weapons along a treacherous
mountain pass. Partisan guides operated and fought
with all six sticks of the SAS Galia force.*

Chapter 6
Forest fireball

As Reg and I stood on that lonely, steep, ice covered road with our hands up, we honestly thought our last moments had come. Then we heard a deep, throaty chuckle followed by a familiar New York accent.

'Hey, fancy meeting up wid you guys way out here. Midnight stroll?'

To our great delight and considerable relief, Pippo Siboldi's cheery face appeared out of the darkness. Major Lett and the small band of walking wounded paratroopers and assorted partisans magically emerged from the shadows a few moments later. We didn't have long to celebrate our good fortune but naturally we were greatly cheered to catch up with the others. They too were delighted to discover that the Captain and the rest of our mates were still at large and were leading the enemy a merry dance.

Our group included seven SAS parachutists – Reg Everett and I, Lofty Rose, Terry Gargan, Pcts Hildage, Kennedy and Corporal Johnson. The two Lofty's (Kennedy and Rose) were in a pretty bad way. Even in the poor light I could make out Kennedy's gaunt, pale, ghost-like face and hunched, shivering body. Although Kennedy was very tall he only weighed about 13 stone. In his condition, he really should have been in hospital not tramping about in the snow-covered mountains. Reg and I divided Kennedy's kit between us and we helped our mate carry on. There was no question of leaving him behind, given his heritage. An Austrian Jew in British uniform captured by the Germans didn't bode well.

Lofty Rose too was suffering from flu or 'mountain fever' as the locals called it but he was a big, thick-set bloke and we had no chance of carrying him, so it was lucky he could still manage to stagger along under his own steam. Hildage's ankle had turned when he dropped into

Rossano. It had been a bad sprain but he could walk pretty well on it albeit he was still in some pain.

Pct. Terry Gargan was also on the road to recovery. He too had been the victim of mountain fever and had been nursed back to health by the local village women who had taken quite a fancy to him. With his shock of curly blond hair, Terry looked more like a teenage choirboy than a hard-bitten parachutist, and old Mama Deluchi (who had made us all a nice cuppa tea on our first day after landing at Rossano), in particular, loved to tweak Terry's cheeks and ruffle his hair, much to our amusement (and Terry's obvious embarrassment). He'd been christened 'the Boy Bandit' by the Rossenesi.

The partisans included an officer, called Avio, a courier Mazzini, a few partisans from Monte Gottero, a partisan named Spartaco and, of course, Pippo Siboldi. A Russian partisan who had been nicknamed (not very originally) 'Ivan' and who had been attached to one of the communist partisan groups had also become attached to our group. None of us were exactly well kitted out, but in comparison to Ivan we were well 'suited and booted'. Poor Ivan's uniform was in rags and he had no overcoat. His feet were bare and encased in sandals held together with string. He must have been in agony from the cold but he never complained. Despite the difficulty we had communicating with him, as he only spoke a few words of Italian and no English, Ivan proved to be a tough, intelligent and resourceful soldier and we all warmed to him and were grateful for his presence. Altogether, our band numbered 14 well-armed men.

The next afternoon Pippo led the way to Sero. We were all feeling the effects of scrambling up and down the slippery, ice-covered tracks and wading through waist-deep snow. As night began to fall we knew we had to find somewhere safe and dry to get some sleep. We came across an isolated farmhouse. The frightened occupant warned us that there were Mongolian ski troops in the next village. He directed us to an abandoned shack about an hour's climb up away up the mountain where he said we could stay the night.

We climbed up the mountain and through the heavily wooded slopes. When we arrived at the dilapidated wooden hut we all crowded inside and the Major posted sentries. Those not on sentry duty settled down for some much needed kip. The shack was built on the edge of a steep gully leading down to the road and afforded us an uninterrupted view of the slopes beneath the trees.

It was nearly midnight when Ivan woke me from a deep sleep for my turn on sentry duty. I took a bit of time to come around. The full moon provided some light. As I rubbed my eyes I could see Ivan and the Major were signalling silently to each other. Quietly I made my way over to the Major who put his finger to his lips and then pointed out of the window. There was deathly silence. We stared out into the gully, looking for movement.

Ivan had spotted it first. On the opposite bank of the gully were two figures in white camouflage snow suits, crawling, commando-style, towards us. Ivan gripped his rifle but the Major grabbed Ivan's arm. He wanted to see what would happen next. As we watched, the two figures silently crawled down into the gully and began to cross the ground towards the shack. When they were about twenty feet away the Major called out:

'*Chi va la*' – who goes there!'

The two commandos immediately turned and scuttled away into the woods as silently as they had arrived.

Ivan and I shook the others awake and helped them gather their kit and weapons. We led the way outside to a more thickly wooded path going further up the mountain. After we'd covered about a quarter of a mile a green Very light shot into the sky and burst above what had been our temporary sleeping quarters. The major did a quick head count and ticked off the men filing past. One was missing. Lofty Rose was not with us. Ivan volunteered to return with the Major to look for him. They had been gone only a few minutes when another green light burst overhead. I called out as loudly as I dared.

'Lofty, Major. Where are you?' There was no answer. I gave a low whistle. The whistle was answered from below.

Mindful that this could have been the enemy we waited silently in the shadows. Presently, a very tall figure staggered into view. By his height and the shape of the dark beret on his head we knew it could only be Lofty Rose. The Major and Ivan followed closely behind. Apparently, Lofty, still suffering the effects of the fever he had contracted, had fallen asleep again momentarily, but had woken just in time to hear us scrambling up the slope outside.

It was a lucky escape, in the nick of time. As the others caught up with us all hell let loose in the woods below. Rapid machine gun fire began to chatter and grenades and mortars exploded. A dull red glow lit up the sky. The wooden hut which had been our refuge a few minutes before, became a blazing fireball in which the enemy had intended we would fry. Tired as we were, this spurred us on to greater effort and we climbed steadily upwards for a further two hours.

Eventually, we reached a clearing in the woods in the middle of which stood a house. Apart from fatigue, we were ravenously hungry for it had not been possible to carry rations. So, Pippo knocked on the door.

After a while a light came on and an old woman answered. Although frightened by the appearance of bedraggled visitors in the middle of the night, she gave us potatoes and other food and told us that the Germans had passed through earlier that day heading for the next village and Monte Gottero. She said they were wearing white uniforms and were on skis. They said they were hunting for three or four hundred English paratroopers.

This was music to our ears, more evidence that the deception plan had worked. The German's were expending scarce resources on a wild goose chase over the mountains for 'hundreds' of paratroopers.

The following day, as soon as darkness fell, we made our way to Pippo Siboldi's village, Sero. Pippo was certain that we would find more partisans there. We knew the enemy only had a short time to carry out their punitive raids and couldn't remain in the mountains indefinitely. By the end of the second day of the valley invasion, they had already begun to withdraw, as they were facing logistical, transport and communication problems. The mules which they, like us, depended on for transport had an unfortunate tendency to disappear in the night, along with the local guides who were press-ganged into leading them from place-to-place. Time, at least to some extent, was on our side, provided of course we remained at liberty and kept on the move.

Our group spent most of the rest of that night moving in stages across a mountain ridge before descending into a small valley. There we took shelter in a house which was already crowded with other refugees, some of whom were partisans from different bands. The prevailing sentiment among this group, however, was one of gloom and despondency. They told us tales of burnings and slaughter by the enemy on a grand scale. We were happy to get out of there and move on at dawn to our next target, a farm over looking Pippo's house at Sero.

At one stage, we had to sit and watch helplessly as a German patrol ransacked Pippo's house before they moved on to the next village, Monte Dragone. Pippo joked that he hoped the 'sons of bitches' hadn't drunk all of his wine!

From intelligence received, it was clear the enemy had been led a merry dance by the villagers. This was their way of hitting back at the invaders who were burning and destroying their livelihoods, their homes and in some cases, murdering their countrymen. The German officer in charge of the troops in Torpiana had spent a disturbed night receiving reports from old men and women with detailed descriptions of where the SAS had last been seen. The officer didn't dare ignore the reports. By daylight his forces were split into numerous small patrols searching for the elusive paratroopers in every direction.

Every direction that is except the right one.

His men returned frustrated, disgruntled, hungry and exhausted. The officer managed to get his men back to HQ by midday only to find half his pack animals could not be accounted for. He was obliged to cease operations and call for re-enforcements.

At last, from our vantage point we could see that Sero was clear of the enemy. Cautiously, we made our way to the village, the full moon lighting our way. Pippo led us to his house and his daughter Lina, made us some hot food which we wolfed down accompanied by Pippo's best wine, which the German's had somehow overlooked.

It must have been around midnight by the time we bedded down for the night in an underground cellar under a barn on the eastern perimeter of the village. We had been on the go for four days non-stop. Sheep and goats clomped around above us but they didn't keep us awake.

After all our exertions and Pippo's hospitality, we slept soundly – blissfully unaware that, as we slept, the enemy had returned in force to encircle Sero, ready to spring their trap.

Chapter 7
Surrounded at Sero

I had the last shift on look-out duty. All seemed quiet outside. Even the sheep and goats in the stable above our heads had settled down. I woke Major Lett and the others as dawn was break-ing. We quickly gathered our kit and a few minutes later, Pippo turned up to lead our group down the track and out of Sero. Pippo was disappointed he hadn't found any more recruits at Sero to join us but that was hardly surprising given the enemy had been there in force so recently. He reckoned the best place to find more partisans was Calice in the neighbouring valley. Major Lett's friend, Lieutenant Dani Buchioni, was the partisan commander there and the Major decided we should head over the mountains to seek his help.

We made our way out of Sero along an icy mountain track moving through the slush and snow as silently as we could, but as always the clack of our hob-nailed boots sounded ominously loud against the eerie, early morning silence. I tried to peer through the thick mist which had swept in across the valley from the sea but visibility was so poor I had trouble keeping sight of the person in front. This was both a blessing and a curse.

On the outskirts of the village we had to cross an open field. When we got half-way, the sky suddenly lit up. A green flare had been fired into the air nearby. We dived flat in the snow as a machine gun opened up on us from the direction of the village we had just left. Another automatic weapon joined in the attack from the front. We were caught in a potentially murderous cross-fire. As we laid there, praying, we could see the tracer bullets passing harmlessly above our heads. It was clear the enemy couldn't see us but were taking a guess as to our whereabouts from the noise we were making.

There was no sense in waiting around for the mist to dissipate. On the Major's signal we made a break for it across the field and into the woods beyond. Both machine guns continued their angry chatter as we bent low and scurried as fast as we could towards the tree line. We could hear the gunners calling out to each other in a foreign language none of us could understand. We realised we had at last come into contact with the Mongolian ski troops we had heard so much about on our travels.

We reached the cover of the trees but were by no means safe. A German soldier, smoking a cigarette, was leaning by a tree. He was so intently peering through his field glasses into the gloom to see what his colleagues were firing at that he didn't see us. As we watched, another German soldier appeared out of the mist to get a light for his cigarette from his colleague. We had no choice but to rush them both and hope there were no others in the immediate vicinity. Lofty Rose and Terry Gargan headed for the first one. Kennedy and I went for the other.

It was all over in a second. They were both so stunned by our sudden appearance out of the mist that they didn't put up much of a fight. After a short scuffle, during which Lofty Rose banged their heads together to quieten them down, they were persuaded to 'come quietly' to meet the Major. They meekly put their hands on their heads and we marched our prisoners the few yards back to the others.

Our captives turned out to be a German Sergeant and his orderly, part of a mortar team. They had orders to open fire on Sero as soon as it got light enough to see the target. The mortar unit numbered eight men in all but their comrades, fortunately for us, took to their heels as soon as we came charging out of the mist. An additional bonus was the fact that the Sergeant had with him a vital part of the firing mechanism without which the mortars wouldn't work.

We had escaped the enemy encirclement of Sero by the skin of our teeth. The enemy withdrawal the previous day had been a feint designed to draw us in. They must have strongly suspected Sero was a partisan stronghold and decided to return during the night to spring their trap. We felt we hadn't done badly in the circumstances by taking two prisoners and getting away scot-free. We now had a chance to make it over the mountains to the comparative safety of Calice. Unfortunately, as we moved through the forest, the early morning mist which had earlier been our saviour, began to lift and we still had the best part of a day's hard slog ahead of us. We consoled ourselves by the fact that if we were spotted, our prisoners would cause confusion and should at least ensure that we would not slaughtered in cold blood.

As the light improved, the sound of gunfire from Sero intensified. We could hear rifle shots in addition to the machine-gun fire but there were no signs of pursuit. A blizzard began and helped mask us from observation from the surrounding heights. An hour later we reached a road which we had to cross before reaching a tall pine forest which we hoped would give us more cover. The blizzard had stopped but the low mist had returned, covering the lower mountain slopes. We could see no sign of the enemy. We crossed the road at the double and entered the welcome cover of the pine trees beyond.

The Major called a halt when he felt we were safe. The sky was very overcast and the icy wind blew the snow off the branches and down our necks. My clothes were sodden. We shivered as we huddled beneath a large clump of rhododendron bushes to take stock. It was the first time since our flight from Sero that we'd had the chance to check our numbers. When the Major counted up we discovered Pippo, Spartaco and Ivan, the Russian who had saved our lives two nights before when he spotted the Mongolian commandos creeping up on us, were missing.

There was nothing we could do. After getting our breath back we continued our journey towards the next valley and the village of Calice. We walked in single file. One of the partisans who knew the route took the lead.

We were crossing a stream when I heard the Major shout a warning to one of the partisans guarding the prisoners. Suddenly a shot rang out. The sound echoed around the valley. I turned and ran back along the line. One of the prisoners – the German orderly – was lying spreadeagled in a stream. He had a bullet hole in the centre of his forehead. The Major was apoplectic with rage at the partisan who had shot the prisoner. There had been a mix up in communication. The Major, worried that the prisoner was about to make a run for it, had warned the partisan guard to keep the prisoner covered. The partisan misunderstood the instruction with fatal results. The whole incident had happened in seconds but in those moments our position had changed significantly. With the German Sergeant as a witness to the shooting of his colleague we could expect no mercy if we were caught. The German Sergeant was standing ashen-faced but with hatred in his eyes. He must have feared his turn was next. We searched him and found he was carrying an identity card showing he belonged to the 285

Grenadier Battalion stationed in Genoa. Under interrogation he told us that his battalion had been rushed in earlier that day as re-enforcements and had reached Sero before dawn, having been transported along the Via Aurelia the night before.

We could do nothing for his dead comrade. We couldn't even bury him decently as it was getting dark and we feared the rifle shot would attract the enemy. We covered his body with leaves and bushes and set off again on the final leg of our journey.

We arrived at the edge of Calice village about two hours later. We didn't know whether the village would be occupied by the enemy so we placed our remaining prisoner at the head of the line to give the impression we were a German patrol. We cautiously moved to the first house on the outskirts of the village. A old man scuttled out of the door and down a nearby lane shouting a warning to other villagers:

'Tedeschi, Tedeschi!'

A woman came out of the house and she too shouted 'Tedeschi!' but then dumped the bucket of water she was carrying and crossed her arms to take a good look at the 'enemy' forces who were about to invade her village. Major Lett grinned at her and explained who we were and that we had come to find Dani Buchione and the Calice partisans. The woman's face lit up and she ran to spread the news to the other villagers. Within a few minutes several men magically appeared from their hiding places. Food and refreshment was produced and while we ate the Major translated as the villagers told him what had happened in Calice.

The enemy had occupied the village for three days and had set fire to the houses and murdered some of the villagers in reprisals. The previous day the troops had all suddenly been withdrawn to go to Torpiana in search of the English paratroopers. The partisan commander for Calice, Dani Buchione, came to meet us and took us into the village itself. A scene of devastation confronted us. Some houses were still burning. Others had been reduced to piles of bricks and masonry.

That night, as we dined on a feast of chicken and potatoes, Dani Buchione received some news from Sero. Two of his men had spent the day gathering intelligence near the village. As we suspected, the enemy had surrounded the village during the night. When we slipped away through the cordon they mistakenly concluded that we had gone to ground among the buildings and cellars in Sero and had conducted a thorough house-to-house search. Then they spotted our boot prints in the snow. The prints were very distinctive and that was how they knew we had been at the village. How we cursed those bloody boots!

When their search for us proved fruitless and they learned the fate of their mortar section, they vented their fury on the unfortunate civilians of Sero. They began shooting villagers at random and killed several, including a young couple and their year-old baby, before a sniper started taking pot shots at them from the church tower.

Pippo Sibaldi, being the tough customer that he was, had decided to double back and conduct a battle of his own. He climbed into the church tower with a rifle and accounted for three of the enemy, managing to escape before the pace got too hot. Nobody new what had become of him after that.

The partisan Spartaco and Ivan the Russian had both been wounded when the Mongolian machine gunners had first opened fire on us. Spartaco had managed to crawl under a bush and was rescued later by Pippo's daughter Lina and other villagers. He was safe, having been carried to a hiding place.

Ivan was not so lucky. He was found by the Mongolian ski troops who duly lived up to their blood-thirsty reputation.

Ivan was still alive, although badly wounded, when they found him. First they blew his head off with a grenade. Then they mutilated what remained of his body, trailing his remains from a tree as a macabre warning to others.

Chapter 8
Reflection and recovery

The Nazis and their *Brigata Nera* allies occupied the valley in force for several days searching high and low for us. Thanks to a combination of good luck, our general standard of fitness, and the fact our partisan guides were able to lead us expertly through forest paths which criss-crossed the mountain slopes, we managed, literally, to keep one step ahead. Towards the end of the *rastrellamento*, the conditions were beginning to take their toll. My teeth were chattering constantly from the biting winds and sub-zero temperatures. Our combat fatigues and woolly jumpers weighed heavy on our backs from the rain, sleet and snow. Fingers and toes suffered the worst – like having strings of frozen sausages attached to each hand and foot. Fiddling about, loading, aiming and firing our carbines would have been nigh on impossible had we come under attack. The only saving grace was that we knew the enemy would be just as tired, cold, wet and miserable as we were, although some of them did seem to be somewhat better equipped for the conditions.

By the end of it some of the lads in our stick had just about reached their 'Waterloo'. Poor Lofty Kennedy, in particular, was in a bad way. He had contracted mountain fever – staggering along like a zombie at a barn dance. He really should have been in hospital not traipsing about in the snow and ice with a raging temperature and hacking cough. He became so ill at one stage that we had a discussion about leaving him behind, hidden in a cave, but he wouldn't hear of it. I could well understand why. None of us would have been in for a comfy ride had we been picked up by the Goons, but an Austrian Jew Commando faced double jeopardy.

In Kennedy's less lucid moments I found myself wearing 6′4″ inches of gangly skin and bone awkwardly draped around my 5′

9″ frame – like some sort of skeletal fox fur (minus the fur) while the other lads carried our kit between them.

Despite the ever-present threat of vicious reprisals, the people of the Rossano valley were typically defiant. The villagers led the enemy troops a merry dance, sending the German patrols on false trails in all directions.

One enemy patrol arrived exhausted at the village of Casa Gaggioli on the night of the third day to find the village deserted and the stores of food well hidden. Of the two mules accompanying the patrol, one had fallen down a mountainside and the other was spirited away by the locals under cover of darkness. The next morning, hungry, cold and disheveled, the miserable bedraggled specimens gave up the unequal contest. On the fourth day most of the enemy troops had been sent across Monte Pichiara to re-enforce the cordon around Sero (which was where we had had to fight our way out of).

Eventually, and luckily for us, the enemy began to run low on supplies. They could not sustain the intensive level of activity. On the fifth day of the occupation of the Rossano valley they, at last, began their evacuation.

News of their withdrawal came early the following day. With two of Dani Buchioni's guides from Calice, our small band, led by Major Lett, once again made ready to move, this time to march back to the valley of Rossano.

As we made our weary way down the slippery, steep mountain paths the sun made a belated but very welcome appearance and warmed the crisp, cold air. We took this as a good omen. We dared to hope that the worst was over and the Gods were smiling on us. This journey, in marked contrast to our more recent adventures, was a cheerful affair. Despite the terrors they had witnessed and the ever-present fear of reprisals, the villagers came out of their houses to cheer us on our way, pressing gifts of food and wine into our grateful hands as we marched past.

As we reached the outskirts of the ruined village of Chiesa we were delighted to find the Captain, Lieutenant Leng and the other sticks who had been playing their own deadly games of hide and seek with the enemy. Incredibly, as far as we could tell, none of our lot had been killed or captured during the *rastrellamento*. Lieut. Riccomini, along with a couple of the other lads who were injured or, like Kennedy, had contracted mountain fever, had been hidden in caves deep in the mountains. We were told they would be brought back into the village as soon as that task could be safely carried out. We exchanged stories and it became clear just how touch and go it had been for some.

Lieutenant Gibbon and Corporal Ford had a particular close encounter: they had a rude awakening when a couple of German soldiers burst through the front door of the house they were holed up in. The pair managed to nip out through the back door, unheard and unseen, to find themselves just outside a cordon of around two hundred enemy soldiers strung out around the village. As they decamped they debated whether to pick off some tempting targets which were standing with their backs to them some 200 yards away. Wisely, they thought better of it, given that had they done so reprisals against the locals, who had sheltered them at such risk, would have inevitably followed.

Later, after our arrival back in Rossano, the villagers declared the day a 'fiesta'. Someone struck up a tune on a concertina and the singing and dancing began.

Over the course of the next few days the partisan forces re-grouped, although they were much reduced in number due to casualties and the capture of many of their number by the enemy. Colonel Fontana, and other members of his staff, had holed up in a cave on Monte Gottero as the Germans searched the area. Lieutenant Leng had stayed with them initially but had then departed and joined up with other SAS sticks. The partisan leader Richetto had been captured in Montegroppo but he escaped before his captors had a chance to interrogate him. Other brigades had split into smaller bands and had scattered towards Parma.

There was no news of the Major's young partisan couriers Nello and Riboncia whom he had sent out to recce the route to Monte Gottero at the height of the *rastrellamento* a few days before. The Major wasn't too concerned at first. They were resourceful lads who were entirely familiar with the terrain. All the same, search parties were sent out to look for them.

We had a few days rest to try to recover from the exhausting ordeal we had been through. Most of us were suffering from illness, fever or ailments of one kind or another related to the extreme weather conditions or poor diet. Lieut. Riccomini and Pct. Sumptor had been brought back by the partisans from their mountain hideaway near Torano. The wireless, which had been buried in a hiding place at Arzelato, was retrieved by Lieut. Leng and urgent messages requesting immediate re-supply of weapons, ammunition, radio equipment, clothing, medical supplies and food were sent to SAS HQ in Bari but, once again, the choice of drop zone proved problematic.

The wireless message had to be sent blind since there was only one-way communications and the radio operator had no way of knowing whether the message had been received. Given the poor physical condition most of us were in, Captain Walker Brown decided to explore whether medical supplies or assistance of some kind could be provided by HQ. A supply drop was requested to be made at the Hunstsville site (Rossano) because the alternative site (Halifax) was still occupied by German patrols at that time.

More in hope than expectation, signals were put out for several days in case the message had got through and supply drops attempted.

Meanwhile, as the days went by with no sign of Nello and Riboncia, the Major grew more and more concerned. Search parties continued to comb the area. On the sixth day of the search they were found.

Nello had two bullet holes in the back of his skull.

Riboncia had tried to escape. His body, riddled with heavy calibre machine gun bullets, lay in a ditch nearby, close to the point they had been told by Major Lett to join the main group after the retreat from Arzelato.

We could see the Major felt the loss of these men particularly deeply. The SAS raid had been his idea and the responsibility and consequences that flowed now weighed heavily upon him. For two years Major Lett had been sheltered, fed and protected by the people of the Rossano valley. He had personally trained and led his partisan brigade in their fight for liberation. Now many of his protectors, the local people and our Italian comrades in arms had paid the ultimate price for their stubborn resistance, their assistance and support. The ruined, gaunt, recently abandoned buildings of what was left of Chiesa following the scorched earth policy of the enemy as they withdrew provided additional melancholy evidence of their sacrifice.

On the 1st February the funeral of Nello and Riboncia took place.

Two chestnut-wood coffins draped with a Union Jack and an Italian flag, which had been used as signals for our parachute drop just a few weeks previously, were carried by pall-bearers from the partisan International Battalion. They marched slowly along into the valley carrying the two coffins containing the bodies of their fallen comrades on their shoulders. All the locals stopped working in the fields and kitchens and lined the edge of the path as the funeral cortege passed by – the men bare-headed and the women weeping. The coffins were placed in the chapel and the Rossenesi filed past to pay their last respects.

The next morning the coffins were taken to the little cemetery below Chiesa for the burial service. We paid these fallen warriors the highest tribute we could. Captain Walker Brown, Riccomini and all of the SAS Galia squad formed a guard of honour. We fell in behind the procession and marched in slow time to the cemetery. Two graves had already been prepared alongside those of the seven airmen who had been killed a few weeks earlier on the ill-fated supply drop.

The village priest, in his sermon, remembered not only Nello and Riboncia but also all the other brave young men of the valley and neighbouring regions who would now not live to see the liberation of their country from Nazi rule and fascist dictatorship. Chella, Nino Siligato and his men, Ivan the Russian and all the innocent civilians who had been caught up in the violence and terror and who had lost their lives.

There wasn't a dry eye in the church – hard bitten SAS commando and swarthy partisan alike. We, the SAS, of course had our own crosses to bare, given the uncertain fate of our comrades who had been captured by the enemy in the first week of the operation. We had had no news of them and feared the worst, especially considering Chella's fate and the Nazis track record of dealing with captured SAS.

With the funeral service over, the coffins were lowered slowly into their graves and the Captain gave the order for us to fire a volley of shots into the air as a last salute to our fallen comrades.

After the sombre funeral service, we needed something to raise our spirits. For several days signals had been put out at the Hunstsville drop zone but the weather remained so bad no-one really expected an attempt to be made. Then, the day after the funeral, the low throb of an aircraft engine could be heard some distance away but coming closer to the valley. The locals quickly completed the, by now, routine for signalling the drop zone to the pilot as the plane came into view.

Despite the signals, the pilot had great difficulty identifying the drop zone due to the thick low clouds that reached half-way down the mountain side. The pilot flew around the Rossano valley for a full hour and a half before finally spotting the signals.

The aircraft made no fewer than six passes over the valley a manoeuvre which had little margin for error. As the plane circled, the crew threw out parachutes attached to which, as we discovered later, were the most urgent supplies requested by the Captain in his wireless message sent a few days earlier.

But that was only the curtain raiser.

Around two hours later, after refuelling back at Bari, the aircraft (a Liberator with two distinctive yellow lightening flashes emblazoned on the fuselage) returned to repeat the same performance but this time, in addition to supplies, the plane dropped a single parachutist. Then, with a dip of its wings in salute to us on the ground, the pilot turned for home and our Liberator disappeared into the cloud for the final time.

We discovered later that this aircraft had been piloted by an American Colonel who was the Squadron Leader at the Leghorn USAAF base. The Colonel was awarded a medal by the British in recognition of his outstanding airmanship and bravery following these supply drops.

Meanwhile, in the valley, we watched the descent of the lone parachutist with some concern. He had jumped from a height of only around 350 feet which was very low and his parachute had also taken what seemed like an age to open. He landed heavily in the deep snow which thankfully helped cushion his impact. We rushed over to the figure who was staggering to his feet as we reached him. The heavy landing had knocked the breath from our visitor's body but he was otherwise OK, although pretty shaken up by his brush with the 'grim reaper'. The contents of his kit bag had fared less well than its owner and had burst far and wide on landing. We set about recovering syringes, tubes of ointment and medicines of all kinds which now littered the floor.

Our visitor was Captain 'Jock' Milne, 2nd SAS Medical Officer from the Royal Army Medical Corps. Captain Milne had been with us on a previous SAS operation in Chatillon in France so we knew him well.

A 'house visit' from a proper army medic was a huge morale boost. Just the tonic we needed to get us back into reasonable shape, ready to resume offensive operations. We would need to be as fit as possible when the time came to make the dangerous journey back through enemy territory, to reach the Allied lines at the end of the operation.

Lofty Rose had the dreaded mountain fever and Riccomini's injured foot had turned septic and he was unable to walk about much. The doctor advised they were unlikely to be fit enough to take part in further operational activities and might have to be left behind to make their own way back across the Allied lines at a later date.

Over the next few days, most of us recovered sufficiently from our various ailments to plan further attacks on the enemy. The Captain had a real bee in his bonnet about blowing up the main railway line which carried enemy supplies to and from La Spezia. We recce'd the track several times but there was no easy way down to access it. We couldn't find a rope long enough to lower our lads onto the line to set the charges. Given our previous experience of blowing up railway lines this outcome was probably for the best. When we were in Scotland, me, Ted Robinson and Spud Murphy (all of whom were part of the Galia squad) were sent by Walker Brown, as a training exercise, to blow up a railway siding. Unfortunately something went slightly awry with our orientation skills. Although we succeeded in our mission, it turned out to be the wrong track. Spud Murphy got arrested by the Home Guard who thought they had bagged a fifth columnist. Walker Brown was not best pleased and had some explaining to do when he found the section of railway line Spud had been carrying as evidence of our 'success' was, in fact a section of track which belonged to the main Glasgow to London express route.

A number of other punitive expeditions were planned and commenced but, in the event, only a couple of further attacks were carried out. This was due in part to the continuing poor weather conditions but also the fact that the element of surprise had been lost. We carried out an ambush on road convoys on the Via Aurellia. We also couldn't resist paying a final farewell visit to Borghetto to attack the enemy headquarters and say our 'goodbyes'. We struck lucky again when some passing Spitfires joined in the attack and strafed the, by now, battered and beleaguered enemy HQ.

Although these raids took place successfully, the ferocity of the enemy reprisals on the local people had taken their toll. We found support from the locals in some areas was beginning to diminish. After further discussion with the medical officer, Captain Milne, in the second week of February Walker Brown signalled his request to SAS HQ in Bari that we be permitted to withdraw from the valley. Quite how that was to be achieved was not clear. We were over a hundred miles from the Allied lines as the crow flies. There were no helicopters in those days of course.

The only way out was along the well-trodden escape line run by the local resistance forces. The terrain we faced was, if anything, even more difficult than the mountains we had criss-crossed to date. The Marble Mountains of Cararra formed a formidable barrier. This mountain range contained peaks rising to over 6,000 feet, higher than Ben Nevis. We would have to scale these at night, in the dark, to avoid the enemy patrols who would be looking out for us. In addition, the Germans had entrenched machine-gun emplacements all along the Gothic Line. To add to the dangers we faced, we were warned by the partisans that all the mountain tracks and paths had been mined.

After all our exertions to this point, we knew this was not going to be a walk in the park. We had no option but to put our trust, once again, into the hands of the local partisan guides who had volunteered to lead us to our destination and pray that our luck would continue to hold.

Walker Brown's account of enemy pursuit

We headed for Rossano, avoiding tracks, but we came into contact with a German patrol. We took two prisoners. One, a Feldwebel, said that there were two German mountain regiments, fascist units, Ukranians and Mongolian ski troops currently engaged in a search and destroy operation for 400 British parachutists. We were suitably flattered!

The situation, however, was very dangerous. The sound of automatic gunfire could be heard all around us. Columns of smoke from burning villages could be seen rising above the hills and mountains. Any village suspected of harbouring SAS or partisans was destroyed. Suspected partisans were shot out of hand.

In one village we went through I saw the bodies of around twenty young men and girls who had been machine gunned to death against a cemetery wall.

At first light, to gain some height advantage, we headed for the summit of Monte Goterro, which is the highest peak in the region at around 7,000 feet. We reached there after a continuous march of just over 59 hours. The slopes of Monte Gottero are steep and our progress was slow due to the heavy snow which had piled up in drifts. The snow was so deep in places it came up to our waists and wading through it drained our energy, especially those leading the column. We had to change the lead every five minutes to keep the pace going.

We had no means of communication. We were running short of rations. We only had one tin of bully beef between two, which of course had to be eaten cold. It was a full ten days before the enemy operation appeared to slacken. Without radio it was now essential to establish contact with Major Lett, his signaller and the four sick SAS men who had been left behind. I sent a couple of my men (Pcts Everett and Hann) to recce the line back to Major Lett. They did not succeed in rejoining the main body for some days. We hoped they had managed to survive but there was a strong possibility that they would have been captured. I led a small patrol which included Lieutenant Leng and a partisan guide on a night-time recce of a mountain village. There was a full moon and plenty of light.

We crept as silently as we were able down a steep, icy mountain track which led into the village. As we got to about twenty yards from the first house someone shouted out a challenge. The shout was followed almost immediately by a long burst of machine-gun fire from the distinctive sounding German MG 42. The burst missed me by inches. We tactfully withdrew.

The next day we found that the enemy had left the area.

We marched back to Rossano to find out whether Major Lett and his party had also managed to evade capture. We had had no word from them since our attack on the Pontremoli road several days before. Using radio, I signalled for a complete re-supply, weapons, ammunition and clothing in order to resume offensive operations as rapidly as possible.

Operation Brake 2
Three of our SAS mates (Pcts Simpson, Ramos and Sergeant Guscott)
who turned up unexpectedly after all the shenanigans with the enemy chasing
us up and down the mountains. They endured an epic and dangerous journey
across the mountains from the Allied side, through enemy territory

Chapter 9
Escape

The Captain addressed us on parade after the response to his request to exfiltrate had been received by courier a few days later from SAS HQ. The intelligence that HQ had received had indicated that we had managed to disrupt enemy plans to such an extent that the troops on the Gothic Line had been significantly affected. This had been borne out by statements made by German POWs taken north of Florence. Referring to Galia's first few attacks on the La Spezia–Genoa road and the enemy HQ at Borghetto in early January, a German prisoner, following interrogation, had said that their offensive in the Serchio valley had not been followed up because of 'unease caused by the Allied raids on the coast'.

Major Farran, our company CO at SAS HQ in Bari, sent a message relayed to us by Walker Brown, saying this was excellent proof of the value of such raids by SAS troops[1] and along with consent to withdraw, he congratulated the whole squad for its fine work.

By the 10th of February, following a final supply drop at Rossano, we were ready to make our move out of the valley. The plan was for us to split into two groups and to make our way out separately within 24 hours of each other to give us all a better chance of making it back. Captain Walker Brown led my group. Lieutenant Riccomini had recovered sufficiently to lead the second group. At 15.30 hrs, the whole SAS troop was assembled in the valley. Captain Walker Brown gave a stirring speech thanking our Italian comrades-in-arms for all their help and to the people of the Rossano valley who had risked and

---

1   *SAS at War 1941–45 by Anthony Kemp, 2000, John Murray, p. 204.*

suffered so much in our support. After Major Lett had translated the speech there were rousing cheers and emotional farewells from the assembled villagers and partisans as our group marched proudly out of the valley for the final time. Old Salvatore, the innkeeper, insisted on accompanying us for the first leg of the journey along with a copious supply of his home-made hooch.

We had been given a point in the Gothic Line to aim for which was supposed to be a space between two German regiments. We had to find this narrow passageway through the strongly held enemy positions to get to the forward Allied American units. We estimated our approach to the Gothic Line would take several days and nights of cautious movement. The Captain, of course, had had experience of this sort of thing before after he escaped captivity in 1943. We knew we would need all his cunning and guile to keep us free of the enemy on this final stage of Operation Galia.

We continued to look for opportunities to attack the enemy as we made our way back towards our lines. After a night in the open, we had to cross the Magra river towards the Aulla–La Spezia main road, which we knew was patrolled regularly by the enemy. Although the road was busy with traffic we saw no sign of any enemy patrol as we crossed. We discussed launching another attack on the enemy communications and supplies but Walker Brown decided it wasn't a practical option as it would be likely to disrupt the POW escape route and would jeopardise the chances of Riccomini's group who were following behind us.

Our first objective to make for was the village of Bibola. This was a fairly steep uphill climb taking us about an hour and a half. A further twenty minutes took us to Vecchietto, where we filled our water bottles at the village spring. From there we began the climb up over Monte Boscoletto (1,917 ft) and on towards Fosdinovo.

We could only carry about two days worth of rations each, one tin of bully beef. We were sick of bully beef and dreamt of the time we could treat ourselves to some proper food. We trudged for miles across the rugged, mountainous landscape making for the town of Vinca. We knew from talking to our guides that this pretty little town, situated at the end of a valley where two mountain ranges meet, had been the scene of an appalling massacre perpetrated by the Nazis and the local fascist militia just a few months before. Over a hundred women and children had been slaughtered as a lesson to others as to what would happen if assistance were provided to the Allies.

From the welcome we received it was clear the 'lesson' hadn't been heeded by these brave mountain folk. The villagers shared what meagre food they had to spare and let us rest up during the day in barns on the outskirts of Vinca. Owing to our sorry physical condition most of us by this stage were unable to carry the heavy weapons for the last stage of the march across the high mountain peak of Monte Altissimo. We gave most of our stuff to the partisans, retaining only carbines and reserve ammunition in order to move forward as a fighting unit. We knew we had to reach the Allied lines soon as we were running very short of rations, ammunition and energy.

We left Vinca at nightfall and pushed on. Fording deep, fast flowing rivers at night was a particularly hazardous and frequent pastime. We had to link arms to avoid being swept away in the current not knowing whether enemy forces were lying in wait on the opposite shore.

An encounter with the enemy did occur on one of these river crossings albeit in somewhat unusual circumstances.

Fording yet another river, we heard giggling and laughing coming from some bushes as we got to the embankment. We crept up quietly and stumbled across a German Hauptman who was found in what the Captain somewhat tactfully described as 'over-friendly contact' with a local girl.

We let the girl go and took 'Lover Boy' prisoner, forcing him to lead the patrol in case we met any more of his friends en route. As we forded the river, however, one of my mates had taken his trousers off and had tied them around his neck to try and keep them dry as he made the crossing. When he reached the other side, he sat down to rest for a minute on what he thought was a low wall. The 'wall' turned out to be a deep well and his trousers duly disappeared forever, into the void. When we took 'Lover Boy' prisoner, our trouser-less trooper (who shall remain nameless to spare his blushes) saw an opportunity to salvage some dignity at the expense of our prisoner who (let's face it) had been caught with his trousers down already.

The Captain wouldn't hear of it.

He had a point. If we were stopped by the enemy our prisoner needed to look the part and say the right things (with Walker Brown's pistol in his back). He would not have looked the part without his trousers. Thus, our comrade became possibly the only man in the Second World War to attempt to cross the enemy lines in his underwear. He knew if we ever got back in one piece, he would never be allowed to forget it.

The serious business of making the transit of the heavily fortified Gothic Line still lay ahead. We planned to make the transit in one night, using old shepherd's tracks. A party of downed American Airmen joined up with us, courtesy of the well-oiled escape route. The partisan guides were reluctant at first to take us through the enemy positions because a mortar position had targeted the escape route the night before. Also fresh minefields had been laid in the area. Despite their misgivings, the guides were eventually persuaded by Walker Brown to push forward.

The march over Monte Altissimo was very tough, dangerous and tiring for all by this stage. Twice we came across enemy patrols but there was no engagement and both groups parted company by mutual consent.

We made the final climb to the summit in the pitch black of night. We couldn't use the mountain track because of the mines which had been laid by the enemy earlier. The climb itself was around 2,000 ft at an average slope of 1 in 4. We reached the pass at the top of the mountain at around 23.00 hrs. Our 'prize' on reaching the summit was to be greeted by heavy enemy mortar fire which fortunately didn't strike a target. At around 11.30 pm we spotted another four-man enemy patrol moving up the track about a 100 yards away. As the advance party, we got into firing position ready to ambush them, but they spotted us and melted away into the dark.

Just before first light, at around 3.00 am on the 15th February we reached what we believed should have been the Allied forward positions. Our prisoner 'Lover Boy' was at the front leading the way. Suddenly, he tripped over a wire which ignited a white phosphorous flare. This should have triggered defensive fire from the Allied lines, but as we waited expectantly in the undergrowth, nothing happened.

We crept cautiously forward. At around 4.00 am, we could see the outline of a small village which we approached as silently as we could. We could see no sign of occupation. Thinking it might not be the right place, I helped to cover the first house we came to with my carbine, while a couple of my mates threw stones at the window to attract attention.

Seconds later a platoon of American soldiers from the US Negro Division came out of the house with their hands up. Their gunners had been asleep and had not seen the trip flare go off. Their commanders were not best pleased when they later learned of this serious breach of security but we at least were grateful to meet our American comrades. After nine weeks of gruelling guerilla warfare, we had finally made it back to our lines in one piece.

Moving to the rear of the Allied lines later that morning we were in high spirits having managed to return without casualties. Then the La Spezia coastal battery, which had 14″ guns that could fire inland, opened up. Two salvos landed nearby and reminded us that we were not completely out of danger even though we were now on the right side of the Allied lines.

Riccomini and his group arrived safely a few hours later.

By the 20th February we were back at SAS HQ in Bari. The achievements and lessons from Operation Galia were still being assessed by the Top Brass but it was clear that the use of a small group of special forces linking up with partisans to carry out attacks on enemy troops, communications and supply lines had been deemed a success both in terms of the results achieved against the enemy and the manner in which the difficulties of weather and terrain were surmounted.

Over the nine weeks of the operation, using 33 men and supplies dropped at Rossano and, of course, taking account of the considerable contribution from the partisans, the tally of damage inflicted on the enemy was significant: 22 trucks and 2 trailers destroyed and 1 truck damaged. Between 100 and 150 enemy casualties inflicted during various actions including attacks on German marching columns and the enemy stronghold of Borghetto.

The enemy had been so harassed and worried by our activities that at the height of the *rastrellamento* the Americans estimated they had used over 6,000 crack troops to sweep the area and search us out. These troops included SS storm-troopers, highly trained specialist mountain troops and a ski battalion.

Galia had also caused major supply problems for the enemy troops on the Gothic Line and caused re-enforcements to be deployed in the search and destroy mission and to re-enforce Borghetto.

This was the first time the 3″ mortar had been used on an operation like ours. The mortar combined with Bren or heavy Vickers machine guns had undoubtedly helped us to take on and engage much larger concentrations of enemy troops, keeping them occupied in battle. Our general level of fitness and training meant that a relatively small number was also able to maintain just enough mobility to shake off the pursuing enemy troops, although more appropriate clothing, especially boots fit for purpose, and proper warm, waterproof, camouflage snow suits would have been useful.

The CO, Captain Bob Walker Brown, was awarded the DSO for his inspired leadership on Operation Galia.[2] Major Lett too received the DSO for, amongst other things, his work behind the enemy lines for SOE and during Galia. The American Airforce Colonel who so skillfully and bravely carried supplies and dropped the medical officer Captain Milne into Rossano for 'house calls', also received a British decoration for his trouble. The Americans repaid the compliment by awarding a US gong to one of us.

We cut cards for it and I think Chalky Wright won. We didn't know at the time mind, but the Yanks medal carried a pension with it, so Chalky did OK out of that. Walker Brown recommended a decoration for the couriers Falco and Ardito in recognition of their services to the force over the past 9 weeks but I am not sure if they ever got it.[3]

Flushed with the success of Galia, Major Farran, CO of 2nd Squadron was keen to launch similar operations as soon as possible to assist the Allied advance.

Events moved thick and fast at SAS HQ even though the end of the war seemed tantalisingly close. Around the time we were making our weary way across the Allied lines to safety, Farran had been busy making the final arrangements for the next SAS Operation in this part of Northern Italy. One of those, Operation Cold Comfort, was an attempt by a small ski-trained SAS party to block the Brenner Pass by creating a landslide.

2 Pro wo 219/5092.

3 Author's note: in the event the British Government, to its eternal shame, blocked any decorations recommended to Italian partisans and these medals were never awarded.

Another SAS Operation – Tombola – led by Major Farran himself would become one of the SAS's most infamous and daring raids of the Second World War but sadly that little adventure resulted in the deaths of two of our Galia comrades so close to the end of the war. For my part, I was selected to drop back into Rossano in April 1945 with eleven other SAS men. Our American allies had failed to press home the advantage by attacking the Gothic Line at the time we were keeping the enemy busy during the *rastrellamento*. Believe it or not, we were ordered to go and do it all over again. Never has an SAS mission been so aptly named – 'Operation Blimey'.

The one thing I wanted an answer to was what happened to Jimmy Church? We had heard nothing since his capture.

I feared the worst.

Our escape route - the forbidding Marble Mountains of Carrara

SAS Operation Cold Comfort

Cold Comfort was launched in broadly the same area as Operation Galia and on the very same day that the men of Galia made it back across the Allied lines to safety.

On the 15th February 1945, an advance party comprising three men were parachuted in behind enemy lines to link up with the partisans. The men were Captain Ross Littlejohn who was new to the Regiment having arrived in the autumn of 1944 from Number 4 Commando, Corporal Dave Crowley and Corporal Clarke. Littlejohn was just 23 but had already been awarded the MC for his fortitude when severely wounded on patrol in an earlier action in France. He feigned death while German soldiers took his watch and other items. He managed to stop himself crying out even after the looters stabbed him in the face with a bayonet. Despite his injuries and perilous position, Littlejohn somehow made his way back across the lines to safety. When he recovered from his wounds he joined the SAS.

Operation Cold Comfort was to be a daring attempt to block the Brenner Pass, which was, by then, the main line of retreat for the German forces (together with many POWs who were forced marched along with them). The SAS was supposed to achieve this by setting off explosions which would in turn create landslides.

Like Operation Galia, was which immediately preceded it, this operation was carried out in atrocious, near impossible weather conditions. As soon as they landed, Captain Littlejohn and Corporals Crowley and Clarke met up with a band of partisans near the town of Pasubio. Once the advance party were satisfied everything was in place to receive the main party they were to signal for the rest of the SAS troop to follow later. The radio signal was duly given to drop the remainder of the SAS party on the 17th February.

---

4   Described in *Stirling's Men*, page 294–5.

But a traitor in the partisan camp had informed the Germans. An enemy ski patrol lay in wait and attacked the reception party as they ploughed through the snow to set up the signals for the pilots to spot at the drop zone. Captain Littlejohn and Corporal Crowley, along with most of the partisans, were taken prisoner but Corporal Clarke and some of the other partisans coming up the rear, managed to escape into the forest.

A few weeks after their capture and only a month or so before the war ended, following interrogation which included SS torture[4] both SAS men, along with a downed American Airman called Charles Parker, were executed. All the men were shot in the back to make it look like they were escaping and were then buried in unmarked graves. The precise circumstances of their treatment and subsequent demise came out at a war crimes tribunal after the war where the SS officers involved were held to account.

Nearly two years before Operation Cold Comfort, members of another SAS Operation, codenamed 'Operation Speedwell', met a similar grisly fate. Pct. Bernie Brunt and Corporal James Shortall were both executed by the Germans for attempting to blow up a railway tunnel, again in roughly the same area of Northern Italy near La Spezia, where Galia later, took place. Lieutenant Pinckney also died on the same mission before his men were captured.

SAS Operation Blimey

There is very little available information about the objectives and achievements of this particular SAS mission which took place in the last weeks of the Second World War following another SAS parachute drop into the Rossano valley. The operation commenced on the 6th April 1945, and was led by Captain Scott, supported by two Lieutenants, Pepper and Wilmers. Each officer commanded three sticks of SAS paratroops. One of these sticks included Galia veteran Parachutist Stanley Hann. It is not clear whether other SAS Galia veterans took part in Blimey but it is possible. At the time of the drop, Major Henderson had temporarily taken over SOE duties in the 4th partisan zone from Major Lett, the latter having left the valley by this time to undertake other duties elsewhere.

Under Henderson's leadership, an attack was launched on Pontremoli on the 15th April 1945 to harass the enemy forces by a joint partisan/SAS force which comprised around a 100 partisans, one stick of SAS plus two officers and two NCOs (Sgts Younger and Hobcraf)] from Mission Blundell Violet.

The SAS and British contingent provided fire with heavy support weapons but the attacking force became outflanked by a German fighting patrol in the hills behind and above the SAS forward position. The SAS withdrew, losing one of the NCOs who was taken prisoner, but who then escaped (in company with his guard) four days later. The heavy weapons were lost to the enemy.

Liberation in this area took place two weeks later on the 25th April 1945. An airstrip was prepared for light aircraft, but never used, since the war by that stage had been won.

Parachutist Stanley Hann was promoted to Corporal on his return. Operation Blimey was his last recorded SAS Operation.

'Behind enemy lines', Italy, 1945. Stanley Hann is at the back, third from right. This is a photograph of the men of Operation Blimey.

Chapter 10
Jimmy Church's story

Operation Galia? I can't tell you much. All that training we went through to get in the SAS. Up and down the Scottish mountains, jumping out of barrage balloons, living off the land.

And for what?

Me and my stick were put in the bag before we'd even seen a bloody German, let alone fired a shot in anger. I remember the journey to the drop zone. In one of those Dakotas. We were all keyed up of course. I never liked flying. That's why I became a parachutist. So I could jump out when I'd had enough.

I sat next to your Dad. Salt of the earth, was Stan. We smoked 30 a day back then and we must've got through a whole packet as we waited for the signal and the green light to appear.

Your Dad and I were close. More like brothers really. We looked out for each other. We had other great mates in the SAS. Lofty Kennedy, Reggie Everett, Chalky Wright, but I only kept in touch with your Dad after the war.

He understood. We didn't need to re-live it. We were both happy enough to move on and to try to forget all that.

On Galia we got put into different sticks. Stan was in number one with Kennedy and the others but I was in number five. Luck of the draw I suppose. Nothing wrong with the other blokes in number five. They were mates too. Trev Harold was our Sergeant and Shaughnessy was the officer in charge. We were the only stick sent south for some reason.

We didn't know who to trust when we landed. We didn't speak the lingo and we had been warned that the place was full of spies and fascist sympathisers so that didn't exactly endear the Eyeties to us. But when we landed we couldn't believe it. The locals were cheering and kissing us like we'd done something special. They made us so welcome it warmed the cockles of yer 'eart. They shared their food even though most of them looked half-starved.

The following day, we were given orders by our CO, Walker Brown, to attack an area around Aulla and Reggio to the south. A young Italian lad was our guide through the mountain passes. Chella was his name. He must've only been about eighteen. Barely old enough to shave. We had little choice but to follow the guides we were given and trust in them. When we reached our destination we were supposed to select targets and attack enemy patrols and marching columns from Modena.

Anyway, our stick travelled all night and most of the next day through snow and ice and up and down the high mountain passes. It was cold enough to freeze the balls of a brass monkey, as we used to say. There were a lot of rivers to cross on the way, most of which we had to wade through. We didn't have any waterproof clothing. When we got wet we just had to carry on regardless.

After a two-day slog we reached a little village called Montebello. It was getting pretty dark and the wind was blowing a gale making the snow pile into drifts. Our guide, Chella, suggested we should rest up in a tumble-down barn for the night and get some shut-eye. We had to ford the river Taro the following morning which, because of all the extra water around, was going to be deep and fast flowing. Lieutenant Shaughnessy thought it would be best to attempt that particular hurdle in the daylight. Since we hadn't seen any sign of Jerry and we were all dog tired and frozen to the bone, it seemed like a good idea.

The old barn we kipped down in was just a derelict stone shack about ten-foot square with only one way in and out. We came across it in the middle of the forest, half-way up a mountain a mile or two outside Montebello. I suppose we thought it would be pretty unlucky for the enemy to stumble across us, in that weather, in that place. Exhaustion probably played a role. Truth be told we probably weren't thinking too straight by then.

I was so knackered I fell asleep as soon as I sat down. The next thing I remember was a lot of noise coming from outside in the early hours before dawn. There was shouting and jabbering in Italian outside and they lobbed a grenade outside the door to show they meant business.

Our choice was simple. Surrender – or be blown to kingdom come.

We found out later there had been what the Italian's called a *rastrellamento*. Their word to describe the way the enemy would suddenly pick an area, flood it with troops, frighten the locals and capture any suspected partisans who were unlucky enough to be there at the time. Turns out that a spy had brought the *Brigata Nera* to Montebello during the night. After searching the village they followed our tracks in the snow and found our hiding place in the woods.

Our captors were all in civilian clothes, not uniforms. When we came out of the shack with our hands up, the trumped up 'Little Hitler' in charge spotted that our lad, Chella, was wearing a small insignia on his tunic lapel showing he belonging to the International Battalion, the local partisan force. That little badge sealed the poor lad's fate. To the fascists, Chella and his partisan friends were traitors. There was no quarter given on either side. Chella must have known what was coming.

He was very brave.

They marched us into the centre of Montebello. They'd got all the villagers out of their beds for a spot of watch and learn. Little Hitler made us run the gauntlet through two rows of his men who roughed us up with sticks and rifle buts as we passed down the line. As Chella got to the end of the line he was seized by two goons who gave him a real going over with coshes and sticks. By the time those bastards were done with him his own mother wouldn't have recognised him. They stripped him of his uniform.

Little Hitler took out his pistol and grabbed Chella by the hair and shouted something in Italian to the watching crowd. Then he shot Chella twice. Once through the head and a second into the body. His body was strung up under a lamp-post in case anyone had any thoughts of helping us.

We thought we were for it next. Instead they loaded us onto a lorry and took us away. None of us knew at that stage about Hitler's Commando Order. We had our suspicions though, and given what they had done to Chella, we didn't rate our chances.

At the prison in La Spezia we were interrogated, separately and together. They beat us with coshes, fists and sticks. It was pretty brutal and basic but at least they didn't try any of that Gestapo malarkey, using electrodes and stuff.

Sometimes they tried a different tack. They would come into the cell at dawn, pull us to our feet, march us outside, tie our hands together behind our backs and put us up against a wall. The firing squad would line up. We were blindfolded and they would ask us one question, over and over again:

'How many?'

Meaning how many more paratroopers were there out there in the mountains.

They only got one answer.

'Thousands and thousands more to come, you bastards!'

After a while the mock executions lost their edge but there was always that element of uncertainty. There were Russians, Poles and Czechs in that prison and, more often than not, they didn't come back.

It was down to Lieutenant Shaughnessy that we managed to survive. He felt responsible for us being captured. He'd been in charge of our stick and had agreed to Chella's suggestion that we should hole up in the shack.

He did all he could to make amends. As long as we weren't handed over to the SS he felt we had a chance. We could see the fascists were worried about reprisals and the possibility of war crime investigations after the war.

So, Shaughnessy proceeded to put the fear of God into them. He told them it was only a matter of time before the war would be over. He made out he was related to Churchill and if any harm should befall any one of his men, he warned they would be hunted down and killed. He told our Italian guards that the partisans and informers in the area had all their names and that he too was keeping track of who was mistreating them. He said the BBC would broadcast the names of war criminals for the Allies to arrest as they advanced.

It was a high risk strategy but his bluff and Irish blarney largely worked and the psychological torture, the mock executions and the beatings became less frequent and eventually stopped. We were pretty amazed that we weren't handed over to the SS who we knew would be desperate to find out the real strength of our forces given we had landed just a few days previously and were now attacking their rear-guard on a regular basis. The SS had tried and tested methods of extracting information from those reluctant to give it.

We were kept at La Spezia jail for about two months. One time we nearly got killed by our own side. Friendly fire they called it. Nothing bloody friendly about a trigger-happy Yank piloting a Thunderbolt.

When the enemy began their retreat we were forced to march back along with them wearing only the rags we had on when we got captured.

Most of us had lost our boots. We had to wrap out feet in whatever we could find. To add to the fun we were chained together – literally – with a ball and chain around our ankles like in one of those American gangster films from the thirties.

We had no opportunity to escape. In any case, none of us by then were in any condition to overpower the guards, let alone run. We were force marched north, up through Italy and across the Brenner Pass, trudging through the snow and bitter cold, all the way into Germany. Many of the blokes in the line got frostbite. We all had blisters and cuts of course. If anyone stopped for a rest or collapsed they were finished. A goon would shoot or stab them there and then by the road-side. That march must've taken us three, maybe four weeks, moving at night to avoid attack from the RAF. Neither we nor the guards had much to eat. We survived largely due to the locals we passed on the way who thrust loaves of bread, chestnuts and potatoes into our hands as we stumbled along.

Lieutenant Shaughnessy, again, helped us to survive.

When we'd gone on the survival training in Scotland, Shaughnessy was always insisting that we should learn to live off the land. He showed us how to forage for food – wild roots, raw vegetables, fruit and berries. We all thought he was off his rocker. 'Oats? Oats?' we said, ''e wants us to eat bloody oats. Only 'orses eat oats!'

For an officer, he was a good bloke and he took all the ribbing in good part.

We had Reg Everett with us in Scotland. Reg was a born poacher and he showed us how to live like kings off the land, shooting pheasants, knocking off rabbits and squirrels. We didn't have to scratch about for berries and roots. We even had venison on that trip courtesy of the kings' highland red deer. Reg wasn't with us though on the forced march. We relied on Shaughnessy's foraging skills. Often we only had to eat what he found for us along the way.

Eventually we reached a POW camp in Germany. We spent the next month there trying to stay alive and recover.

We were liberated by the advancing American forces in April 1945. I was hospitalised for a time after they got me out. I remember the American nurses. To us, they all looked like angels sent from heaven. Gorgeous they were. I was repatriated in late April 1945. I weighed around eight stone, about half my normal body weight.

The end of the war came a week or two later.

I don't remember being debriefed. I was de-mobbed along with thousands of other returning soldiers. The SAS was disbanded. I had to look for a job in civie street after five years of being a soldier. No one had heard of post-traumatic stress disorder back then. No treatment from psychologists or counsellors. I don't think we would've taken it anyway.

I didn't go to the SAS reunions. Your Dad went to a couple but I would never go. I didn't collect my campaign medals either. Didn't feel right somehow. I didn't deserve 'em. I never fired a shot in anger.

Author's note

Jimmy Church's stick were captured on 1st January 1945, less than a week after landing. By the end of Operation Galia it is estimated over 6,000 enemy troops were searching for the SAS, believing a much larger force than the 30-odd men that had landed and were attacking them. The deception had worked, thanks in no small part to the fact that none of the six SAS men captured gave way under interrogation to reveal the true number of men comprising the Galia force.

Chella Leornardo and his memorial (© Brian Lett).

PART TWO

Epilogue:
the author's story

*'I knew your father'. Rob Hann shakes hands with Lino Moggia,
a veteran partisan fighter who was just 18 when the SAS forces were dropped
behind the German Gothic Line defences. Two of Moggia's relatives were
murdered during Nazi reprisals.*

*My father in his milkman's uniform after the war
in Winchmore Hill North London*

When, as a lad, I asked Dad anything about his wartime experiences, he would typically shrug his shoulders and say something nonchalant like:

"Oh I parachuted down, made a nuisance of myself and then ran about a lot, chased by the enemy."

That was how I learned he had been in the SAS. Apart from a few sketchy 'war stories' – Dad mentioned once, for example, that he had once hidden in a cabbage patch just feet away from the boots of German soldiers – this was as far as my knowledge of his war went. Where he had served and what he had done in the SAS was a complete mystery to me.

The "Dad" I knew was a gentle, family man who worked extremely hard to provide a decent life for his wife and three sons. Stanley Hann had been a milkman before he joined up in 1941 and took up where he left off after the war ended. He did his milk round – rain, snow or shine - for the rest of his working life. His boys took it in turns, as we grew up, to help him out, for pocket money and tips, at weekends and school holidays, to deliver milk to the doorsteps of Winchmore Hill, North London.

In 1984 my parents moved to Frinton-on-Sea, Essex (where my Mother still lives) to enjoy their retirement. Dad's friend and former SAS comrade, Jimmy Church (always known to me as "Uncle Jim") and his wife, Winnie, moved from their flat in Bermondsey, to live near them in neighbouring Clacton.

In 1993, Dad's wartime comrade, Eric (Lofty) Kennedy, came over from his adopted home in Canada, to stay with my parents for a few days. Kennedy had come to England in order to attend the SAS's 50th anniversary celebrations in Colchester, where a dinner was being held in honour of the SAS 'originals'. To my (now) eternal disappointment, I didn't take much notice at the time. About the only thing I remember was that, try as they might, neither Kennedy nor Dad could persuade Jimmy Church to attend the re-union with them.

Occasionally, it's true - Dad would open up about the funny stories and pranks he and his mates had got up to in SAS selection, parachute training or on leave, but, like so many of his generation, he would never go into detail about the Operations he had been on. I put this reluctance down to the fact that the SAS was a notoriously secretive organization and that Dad had probably sworn never to reveal the details of the missions he had been on. That suited both of us then - but now, with the benefit of hindsight, I don't think his silence had anything to do with SAS secrecy. It was much more complicated than that.

How could he explain to his children the reality of war? How could he sanitise for decency's sake, the destruction, the maiming, the killing and the misery that he must have encountered, been part of or, perhaps, held himself responsible for when fulfilling his duties? How could he do this without making it all appear like an incredibly exciting adventure, thereby potentially glorifying the war to his children who he hoped and prayed would never have to face the same sort of reality he had faced? Dad's perfectly sensible solution was to remain silent and to 'move on'. He didn't want to relive the war or to live in the past or brag about what he had done. He used to say "I did my bit, like a lot of others at that time," and that was that.

Of course, I always hoped he might sit me down one day and explain it all to me, perhaps when I was older, more able to understand what, specifically, his 'bit' had been.

But he never did.

My Father died in November 2001, a few weeks after celebrating his 80th birthday. His death was sudden, unexpected, completely devastating for my mother, his sons, friends and family, as these things inevitably are. He had been ill the year before with the big 'C'. We all thought he'd beaten it, but Cancer did what the Nazis couldn't do all those years ago.

Ironically, it was only then that I began to learn more about Dad's war. The day after his funeral, Jimmy Church, took me aside and told me that Dad had been the greatest friend a man could have and then told me at least some of the answers to the questions I had been asking.

Jimmy confided that he and Dad had once taken part in a dangerous SAS mission in the mountains of North-west Italy during the harsh winter of 1944-45. Jimmy had been in a separate 'stick'. He and his comrades in his stick had been captured in the first week of the mission. Jimmy, understandably given the circumstances, became very emotional when he told me what happened when he had been captured. His experiences as a POW clearly still affected him, despite the passage of time. In typically British 'stiff upper lip' fashion, it seemed Dad and Jimmy had not spoken much to each other about their respective experiences after the war, preferring not to dwell on such disturbing memories.

For me, Jimmy's story both fascinated and tantalized. To be told that my Dad had parachuted into action, behind enemy lines on a dangerous war-time mission just did not fit the memory of the "Dad" I had known all my life. I was desperate to know more but, at that time, the demands of work and my young family – two lively boys, William and Joseph – took priority.

In the autumn of 2005, Jimmy died. His death affected me greatly. I also thought my best chance of learning anything more about Dad's secret war had gone. But Jimmy's widow kindly gave me some mementos. Included among them was a dog-eared, team photograph of a number of men in battledress in front of a Dakota. On the back was inscribed 'Operation Galia, Northern Italy 1944/45'. I picked out both my Dad and Jimmy easily among the thirty odd paratroopers in the photograph - the first real clue to unlocking Dad's wartime secrets.

My Mother had a box number address for the SAS and so I wrote a letter asking for any information they may have about SAS Operation Galia. I was staggered when I received through the post a few weeks later, an eighteen-page operational order and a detailed contemporaneous report containing dates, times, people, places of 'Operation Galia' by its commanding officer, Captain Bob Walker-Brown. Dad was mentioned by name several times in the report and it became clear that he had been involved in some very heavy fighting, covered great distances in hostile weather conditions and had faced extreme danger.

Again, I desperately wanted to find out more, but within the space of a few weeks of Jimmy's death I had my own demons to face.

I became seriously ill with what was later diagnosed as a particularly aggressive form of arthritis. This type of arthritis (there are many apparently) attacks the major joints. I had never been ill before and had regarded myself as being a reasonably fit 'forty something'. I now struggled to walk a few hundred yards to take the kids to school. In intense pain I learned that the disease had already attacked and almost destroyed my left hip. My right knee had also been affected. The specialists told me that my hip would have to be replaced but that couldn't be done for at least a year. After a lengthy spell in hospital, the condition was temporarily stabilized by medication. In the meantime, until surgery could be carried out, I had to get around with the aid of crutches or sticks.

Thus, somewhat low in spirit, mobility impaired and partially dependent, I needed to find something positive I could focus on which didn't take a great deal of physical effort. Researching Dad's role in 'Operation Galia' turned out to be just the therapy I needed. With modern communication and research facilities I was but a 'click' away from a world of information and discovery. Now I had the name of Dad's SAS mission and Walker Brown's debrief report, the World Wide Web helped me to discover more and more about Galia. My Mum got into the swing of things and helpfully dug out some wartime photographs of Dad in snow-clad mountains with some of his SAS comrades.

I learned of an annual walk along the north Italian escape routes used by Allied PoWs and parties of SAS and made contact with the organizer, Brian Lett. I discovered that Brian's father, Major Gordon Lett, had been an escaped British PoW who joined SOE and established a British Mission, code-name Blundell Violet, centred in the Rossano Valley, the same valley my father had parachuted into. The local villagers had adopted Gordon Lett as one of their own and he had quickly become the lynchpin of British SOE operations in the area. It was Major Lett who organised the mixed band of partisans and foreign fighters into the Battaglione Internazionale to harass local Nazi and Fascist forces and to assist Allied PoWs to escape. I had learned from reading the report on 'Operation Galia' that it had been Gordon Lett who had welcomed and briefed the SAS when they landed in the Rossano Valley.

Brian Lett had already done a tremendous amount of research and he assured me that our fathers must have known each other and had shared at least one potentially fatal encounter with the Germans in a tiny ridge top village called Sero. Brian organised the San Martino Freedom Trail, an annual event which, since 2001, has raised funds for the Monte San Martino Trust, a charity founded in 1989 by Keith Killby OBE and other ex - PoWs as a permanent tribute to the Italian people of the region who aided so many escapees. The Trust provides bursaries for young Italians to travel to England to improve their English.

The Freedom Trails attract walkers from around the world, keen on following the PoW and SAS escape and 'exfiltration' routes across the mountains of northwest Italy to the coast on the Gulf of Genoa. Brian told me that part of the summer 2006 Rossano Freedom Trail would commemorate the success of 'Operation Galia'. The thought of visiting Italy and following in Dad's footsteps in the company of someone as knowledgeable as Brian was too great an opportunity to miss.

I was still not fit or mobile enough to take part in the entire week long walking expedition, but I was nevertheless determined to honour my father's memory by taking part somehow. I set myself the target of walking selected parts of the trail with my family (Stanley's grandsons) visiting the main battle sites and, perhaps, meeting some of the veteran partisans involved.

Rossano 2006

And so, in July 2006, my family and I took a flight to Parma, picked up a hire car and drove south along the Autostrada as it snaked its way high up into the stunning green beauty of the mountains of the Northern Italian Apennines' on our way to the Freedom Trail base in the city of Pontremoli. There we met up with Brian Lett and the rest of his walking party, including guest-of-honour veteran PoW escapees like Mick Wagner and Jim Bourne, the descendants of partisan families who had sheltered Brian Lett's father, the British Consul based in Florence and other people who, like me, had their own reasons for coming on the trip, from Britain, Italy, Canada and South Africa.

The next day I attended a ceremony at a memorial to all anti-fascist forces and to the memory of Major Gordon Lett, high on a mountainside overlooking the Rossano Valley at Pradenilara. There I stood for the first time and gazed over the sun drenched valley, flanked by high, chestnut tree clad mountains, to the spot where the Galia squadron had parachuted into Rossano sixty four years earlier. Brian Lett pointed out the drop zone (code named 'Huntsville' in Walker Brown's debrief report) – a tiny patchwork of terraces tumbling down a mountainside over to the southwest - at which his father, Major Gordon Lett had first greeted the SAS on their arrival. The terrain looked daunting enough to me in high summer, but I had to wonder how my father and his comrades had summoned the courage and faith to jump from an aircraft in midwinter into this tiny 'bowl' with all

---

1   Keith Killby is a remarkable man of 97 at the time of writing whom the author has had the pleasure of meeting several times in recent years. Keith was an SAS 'original' but was also a contientious objector who was given special dispensation not to carry arms. Keith was attached to the medical corps in the SAS and was captured and escaped several times whilst on active duty. His life and adventures would make a fascinating story in its own right.

identifying features shrouded in snow.

From the vantage point near the memorial it became clear how one American pilot had crashed into the mountain-side, killing all personnel on board and, in the process, creating huge logistical problems for the men of Galia, when the USAAF refused to drop supplies into the Rossano Valley thereafter.

Later we moved down the mountain to the village of Castoglio and at an emotional meeting I was introduced to Antonio Deluchi and his daughter Serena who had been one of the beneficiaries of a bursary from the Monte San Martino Trust. Antonio is the son of Tarquinio Deluchi, a partisan who sheltered Gordon Lett as his own son from September1943. Antonio pointed towards the dappled terraces behind us, 'they landed over there' he said, 'and it was my mother - Serena's grandmother - who welcomed your father with a cup of tea as soon as he had landed.'

The following day we joined the rest of the walkers at the village of Pieve to march the final stretch into the village of Sero. Brian allowed my two boys to carry an original banner of the Battaglione Internazionale, as we symbolically 'liberated' Sero once more. This had been the village in which the Germans had trapped several men including my father, Gordon Lett and several partisans on the 21st January 1945. It was here that I discovered Dad's 'war story' had been true all along. The cabbage patch in which he hidden to evade the enemy search parties sent to kill him was situated on a hillside in Sero.

I was introduced to several veteran partisans – Dino Paoletti (a former Partisan leader), Lino Moggia, Alberto Siboldi (a descendant of the partisan leader Pippo Siboldi) and Aldo Farina - who had all been teenagers when the SAS dropped into their valley.

Lino Moggia despite the language barrier, was keen to regale me with the story of those fateful days in Sero long ago. He was a great character. A sprightly 80 year old with a solid bare, bronzed chest, piercing steel blue eyes beneath a shock of white hair, he led me on a tour of the partisan bolt-holes in the ancient hilltop village pointing out where the SAS had stored their ammunition and weaponry when they used the village as their battle HQ. As if to underline his indigenous credentials, Lino had a sprig of rosemary poking out of the corner of his mouth – as if he was smoking a very thin, badly rolled cigarette. Half way round, the grizzled partisan veteran suddenly gripped my arm and, fixing me with a penetrating glare, turned my face to one side and nodded sagely.

'I knew your father' he said, 'you look so much like him'.

An astonishing moment. There was no doubting Lino's sincerity, but could he really have remembered what Dad had looked like after all these years? Dad would have been just one of thirty-odd SAS soldiers in uniform.

It didn't really matter. What Lino Moggia had said and the way he had said it, was thrilling and for me completely justified the effort I had made to explore Dad's story this far.

Listening to the passion of the veteran partisans as they talked of those dark times of 1944-45 is to discover that 'Operation Galia' and the events surrounding it still resonate in this region of Italy. That evening, as I stood side by side with some of the men who had fought with my father, Brian Lett mentioned my Dad's name during a ceremony at the memorial to those partisans killed in the Nazi attack on Sero. It was another very emotional and proud moment for me. Dad would certainly have been very surprised that he and his comrades were still remembered and commemorated here all these years later.

But Brian had one final treat in store for me. To round off my day he put me in touch by mobile phone call to the UK, with Lieutenant Colonel Bob Walker-Brown, commander of the Galia mission.

'Your Dad was a fine soldier' he said, 'I remember him well.' Speaking to Dad's former commanding officer at the scene of Dad's closest brush with death was another incredibly emotional experience for me.

Two days later we traveled to Montebello in Mezzo where Jimmy Church had been captured and their partisan guide, a young man called 'Leonardo Chella', had been murdered in front of him by the fascist Brigate Nera. Knowing Jimmy personally and the strength of his bond with my father, this was a special place for me. I searched for and found a memorial to Chella in the village and paid my respects to a courageous youth. Later, I found another monument to Chella erected above an old cascina. Knowing that the partisans erected monuments very close to where the events they commemorate occurred, it was at least possible that this barn could have been the cascina in which Jimmy was sheltering when he and his comrades were captured in the early hours of New Years Day 1945.

Later that day, I was privileged to meet another former partisan, Dimmo Baldossin who I discovered had parachuted into Rossano as an Italian liason officer, along with my Dad on a subsequent SAS mission, code named "Operation Blimey" in late March 1945.

I had found out so much more about what my father had been involved with in Italy thanks to the partisan veterans and Brian Lett. I wanted to come back again when I was fitter and was able to take part in the commemorative walks. So, even as we took our leave, I made plans to return to Rossano the following year.

Rossano revisited – August 2007

My second visit to Rossano took place almost a year to the day since the first. Brian Lett was kind enough to allow our family to stay in his holiday home, a converted school house in the centre of Chiesa di Rossano. The accommodation, which is known as 'the Centro', overlooks the Rossano valley. The Deluchi family, Lina and Antonio, live next door to the Centro and greeted us like old friends. Our two boys watched open-mouthed as Antonio proudly and tangibly demonstrated his partisan heritage by fetching a number of relics from the war he had found tucked away in his loft:

- a pair of German Army binoculars;
- a live round from a Vickers machine gun;
- an ancient *Carabinieri* revolver with the firing pin removed; and (most impressive of all – to me at least)
- an ancient hob-nailed boot complete with parachute chord laces.

Could this have been one of the boots worn by an SAS parachutist? Worn by my Dad?

The Deluchis gave us the key to the Centro and bade us welcome.

That night when the kids were safely tucked up, I stood on the veranda of the Centro with a glass of Chianti and gazed out at the steeply sloping hill sides of the Rossano valley below. The full moon lit the scene. The incessant chirping of the cicadas and a barking dog somewhere in the village were the only sounds to interrupt the peace and tranquillity. Had life in this out-of-the-way spot changed in the sixty-odd years since the SAS made their dramatic and unannounced entrance?

The following day we made our way down the steep mountain paths out of Chiesa to the nearby village of Coroletta towards Bosco. We walked along the 'Via Gordon Lett', the only visible memorial in the village to the man who was responsible for Dad (and now me) coming to this remote corner of Northern Italy. Our lads splashed in a fresh, cold mountain stream which babbled at the valley base over rocks, boulders and stones creating cascading waterfalls in some parts and natural swimming pools in others where the boys could safely practise their crawl and breast-stroke.

Later, the boys and I paid a visit to the village of Arzelato, which, thanks to its high church tower and commanding, panoramic views over the valley, had played such a crucial role on Galia. Arzelato is situated high up in the Appuan mountains, half-way between Rossano and Pontremoli. There we met up with Brian Lett and his family.

We found the church tower easily enough and the views over the valley below even from its base were breathtaking. However, the climb to the top of the tower – up three woodworm-riddled ladders propped almost vertically against the church wall – was hair-raising. These must surely have been the original ladders the commanding officer of Galia (Captain Bob Walker Brown) and Brian's father (Major Gordon Lett) had climbed to survey enemy troop movements far below and where they had planned their guerrilla offensive.

As we reached the summit it was easy to see why Arzelato had been such an important place to the SAS. The town of Pontremoli lay deep in the valley basin. This was the enemy HQ in the region during the occupation with the main roads and railway to La Spezia forming the all-important communications and supply routes to the Gothic Line defensive positions established by Kesselring. Here the officers planned and executed their lines of attack with the partisan commanders whose men led the SAS into battle and spirited them away after their attacks.

The incredible thing to me was that the church tower remained intact and undamaged. For some reason, even though they must have known its value to the SAS, the Germans did not destroy or even attempt to shell the church tower. In January 1945, Captain Bob Walker Brown, in his battle report, mentioned how, from this vantage point, he managed to spot through his binoculars enemy ski troops dressed in winter camouflage and carrying skis, fast approaching. The only reason he was able to pick them out was the fact their snow suits, being mud-splattered, stood out against the snowy backdrop. The SAS beat a hasty retreat down these rickety wooden ladders and decamped over the snow-clad mountain trails to fight another day.

As the boys and I took our leave of the tower summit we gingerly clambered down. Masonry and cement followed in our wake and we prayed the rungs would hold firm one more time. Safely on *terra firma* the villagers treated us to coffee and cakes in the narrow, steep road leading up to the church. Just at that moment the bells in the tower began to chime. The 'bong, bong, bong' of the bells were deafening in the small narrow streets and we were glad we had made it down from the tower before they started. No-one had thought to warn us about that particular hazard.

A few days later came the highlight of the trip for me. I was going to walk the route taken by the SAS when they retreated from Arzelato at the height of the January 1945 *rastrellamento*. This was the first time I had been fit enough, since my illness, to undertake such an arduous, physically demanding hike. The paths, little more than tracks really – once well-trodden by man and beast alike – were now overgrown. The going underfoot was hard, rough and boulder-strewn. At least, this being August, we didn't have the snow and ice to contend with and hob-nailed boots, thankfully, were not in fashion.

Mules would have been the main form of transport through the mountains in the 1940s, indeed for centuries before then. A tarmac road now allows vehicular access to these remote villages, so the need for pack animals has declined but mules have not entirely disappeared from Rossano. A grumpy farmer met us half-way down one of the tracks. His mule had disappeared and he was frantically searching the forest for any sign of the beast. We promised to keep an eye out for it and both parties went on their way.

Our guide through the mountain tracks was one of the last remaining chestnut flour millers in the valley, Giovani Tongnatelli. Giovani, who was now in his late seventies, had been a boy of thirteen during Galia. He had known Brian's father, Major Lett, very well and had often hidden him and brought him essential supplies when danger threatened, at great personal risk to himself. The elderly miller took great pride once again, in leading his British charges along the thickly wooded tracks, sometimes journeying entirely 'off-piste' to link up with other uncharted routes, which only he, with a lifetime of experience in these mountains could have known about.

As we tourists slipped, sweated and grumbled about the heat and gradients, the seventy-something Giovani led the way, fresh as a daisy in his clean white shirt and his grey flannel trousers, looking more like a bank manager on an away-day. I never saw him so much as sip a drop of water or break into a sweat as we struggled along behind.

In a remote part of the forest, deep in the valley, Giovani led us down to a fast flowing river bank to what had been his father's mill. The mill had been standing on the site since the fifteenth century but had fallen into disrepair a few years after the war. It was not the only casualty of the decline of the local industry. All over the forest we had come across abandoned buildings associated with the chestnut flour industry. Giovani was one of the last of his kind with a working mill in the valley. Chestnuts which, back home, would cost a small fortune in Marks & Spencer's, littered the forest floor, serving only to sprout new trees, and make access to the tracks even more difficult in the future.

The old mill was in a severe state of decay and dilapidation. Two huge mill-stones, looking like giant polo-mints, stood guard outside what would have been the main entrance. Curiously, the door was propped ajar as if Giovani's father had popped out for few minutes to collect chestnuts. A glance inside the dark, foreboding interior dispelled any such romantic notions. No-one had ground chestnuts into flour here for a very long time.

As he showed us around inside the dangerously unstable ruins, Giovani told us how he and his father had hidden Major Lett and other POWs during a search led by the *Brigata Nera*. In one corner some homemade chairs and tables were stacked against a wall. The miller told us they had been made by escaped prisoners of war whom he and his father had hidden. Anywhere else in Italy an old water mill in a picturesque setting, which charted the social history of the area and which contained actual relics from a Second World War adventure story, would be made into a money-spinning heritage trail. Here, its remoteness and decrepit condition made renovation an impossible dream.

As we rested in a clearing, near the ramshackle mill, we listened captivated as Giovani told us how, one day, he had hurried to the mill when the woods were being searched by the *Carabinieri*. He and his father moved the Major and the other escaped POWs to a safer place. When he returned to the mill he was seized by two *Carabinieri*, one of whom pointed a pistol to his head and threatened to shoot him unless Giovani told him where he had hidden the British Major. Giovani said (modestly) that he was too terrified to speak and the policeman holding the gun said to his comrade: 'Well, shall I shoot him then?' And the other replied 'No, let him go. I know him. He's a good lad.'

On such slender threads, life was balanced in those dark, dangerous days.

So we left the old mill and its memories and secrets and continued to follow the ever-sprightly old miller along the mountain tracks to arrive safely back to Galia HQ at Rossano.

The final day of our visit we drove our hire car to Pieve, a mountain-top village deep in the Ligurian countryside. Here we met up with Brian Lett and the other walkers to march the short distance into what was the heartland of the partisan resistance movement in this region, the home of the partisan leader Pippo Sibaldi and Galia battle HQ – the village of Sero. Brian Lett led the way into the village carrying the original *Internationale Battalian* flag of his father's partisan group. When we reached Sero we were met by some of the same partisans who had turned out to meet us the year before. One of them, an excitable 89-year-old called Aldo Farina, told us how the German's had thrown a cordon around Sero before launching an attack, in a vain attempt to trap some of the SAS men (my father included). During the attack an entire family – mother, father and baby – had been machine gunned to death. Their names were engraved on a memorial in the centre of a wall of the first building in the Sero market square.

Later, I took a short stroll to the cemetery which is situated just outside of Sero. There I found the family, their graves still tended with fresh white lilies. It was a sobering moment. The date engraved on their tombstones (21st January 1945) was a powerful reminder of the dramatic and tragic events of that day.

I hoped to find some evidence at the cemetery of 'Ivan the Russian' who had been killed when Major Lett, my Dad and their comrades made their escape from the enemy encirclement at Sero. Last year, another octogenarian partisan veteran, Lino Moggia, told me that he remembered my father because I looked so much like him. Lino also told me how Ivan the Russian had been badly wounded but was still alive when the German's found him. Lino spared me none of the gory details of how the German's had despatched poor Ivan using a grenade and how they then set about mutilating his remains. The villagers had apparently buried what was left of Ivan's body in the Sero churchyard. I was looking for some memorial to him, but I could find no evidence of Ivan sixty years later.

I did, however, meet up with Lino Moggia again.

Lino's unmistakable image, a sprig of rosemary poking out of the corner of his mouth, beamed out at me from his freshly laid crypt. I had missed him by about three months. Sadly, this year the only partisan I met was Aldo Farina. All the others, like Lino Moggia, had passed on or were too ill to make this year's rendezvous.

There was one more discovery waiting for me, though, at Sero, when I returned from the cemetery.

The owner of the local bar, Alberto Siboldi, was a descendant of the local partisan hero Pippo Siboldi. After honouring his visitors with a barbecue and drinks he led us on a tour through the narrow streets which honey-comb the centre of Sero. He showed us where Galia had set up their battle HQ. A three-storey, detached house with green shutters set apart from the rest of the village with easy access to the surrounding countryside in case a quick exit was needed. He then led us along the old part of the village, through some dark alleyways and into a basement of a building which was in the process of being renovated as a holiday let for an absentee landlord.

There, Alberto told us that this had been a barn in 1945 where sheep and goats were kept during winter. Major Lett, my Dad and the rest of the SAS stick, partisans and assorted allies, had been sleeping in the room below as the village was surrounded and then attacked on the early morning of 21st January 1945. Apparently the Germans had known the SAS forces were in the village, since they had spotted their distinctive boot-prints in the snow.

How Dad and his pals must have cursed those boots!

Four unfortunate villagers paid the ultimate price for sheltering the SAS but a plaque in the village square records it could all have been so much worse. After Major Lett's group had escaped, the Nazi storm-troopers and their allies rounded up all remaining villagers into the village square, intent on exacting retribution. Fortunately, the village priest managed somehow to successfully trade the lives of the villagers for food, supplies and mules, which had been hidden from the invaders. A massacre was somehow avoided thanks to the priests' brave intervention.

That final evening I wandered for the last time around Sero. The full moon lit my way and, as in Chiesa, the only sounds to disturb the peace were the chirping cicadas and the barking dogs.

I realised I had been lucky to at least discover something of what went on here all those years ago before the last original memory passed away. Time, inevitably, is drawing a curtain across this turbulent history.

But thanks to Brian Lett's organisational skills I had one more opportunity to explore an aspect of Galia which sounded exciting and challenging. Brian told me he was planning to lead a small expedition to walk the tough and dangerous freedom trail which was much used during the Second World War by escapers seeking to cross the German Gothic Line in Northern Italy in order to reach the safety of Allied lines. The Gothic Line ran south of the Magra valley, running through the almost impenetrable Marble Mountains above Sarzana, Massa and Carrara. For escapers arriving from north of the Magra, it was a most demanding challenge.

So in September 2007 I found myself, once again, on a flight bound for Parma and ultimately Rossano. This time I was on my own without the family. This was a challenge I faced with a peculiar mix of excitement and trepidation. I wondered briefly whether I would be fit enough for such an undertaking given only nine months previously I had had a hip replacement. Could I really walk my father's escape route, over the 6,000 metre peaks of the Carrara Marble Mountains? I consoled myself with the knowledge that at least I had done some walking in the Rossano mountains.

How difficult could this challenge be?

The Escape Trail – September 2007

Brian gave me fair warning that this would be a hard, no frills, no ceremonies, trek. Twice before Brian told us he had tried and failed to complete the journey. He had organised a very strong party to attempt the trail in April 2003. His then group of 36 had included 6 'Smiths' from 21 SAS and 18 'Browns' from 23 SAS. An unexpected and unseasonal heavy fall of snow on the first day of the trail frustrated the attempt. Brian said his advance planning had proved wholly insufficient to overcome the problems his party had faced. He ended up walking no more than a third of the trail.

Undaunted, in May/June 2004, he tried again. This time, he did not have any military participation. Again, he didn't complete the journey due to the weather. He had to abandon his attempt on Monte Altissimo. We were to undertake the journey at the best possible weather conditions, in September. The intention was to travel without transport or back-up crew. If we failed to complete the trail in four days, Brian's cunningly simple fall-back plan was for us to continue until we finished on the fifth day. Flexibility was to be the key to success. We were to walk from Chiesa di Rossano to Serravezza a distance of over eighty miles as the crow flies. Given that the terrain we were covering was exceedingly mountainous, it was clear this would be no stroll. Between the summer of 1944 and April 1945, hundreds of escapers found their way through with the help of Italian guides. The escape trail twisted and weaved its way through enemy positions, changing when necessary from month to month. Our aim was to follow as closely as possible the exfiltration route used by Operation Galia as documented in Bob Walker Brown's de-brief report.

The men of SAS Operation Galia had left the valley of Rossano at 15.30 hrs on 10th February 1945, having fought a guerrilla campaign behind German lines since 27th December 1944. They had arrived at the Allied Front line at 03.00 hrs on 15th February 1945. They had spent the night of 11th/12th February scouting the area around the town of Aulla in the hope of finding targets, before deciding to exfiltrate. They faced heavy snow, mined trails and enemy patrols but they made it through eventually to the Allied lines. History had therefore shown it was, at least, possible to do this trek in four days.

In retrospect, perhaps I should have paid a little more attention to some obvious distinguishing features between my Dad and me. For example:

1. I have never been in the SAS.
2. I am a soft-bellied lawyer approaching my fiftieth year.
3. My Dad was a 23-year-old, highly trained commando in the peak of physical condition (albeit suffering from the effects of malnutrition, seven weeks of guerilla fighting and freezing weather).
4. Even at my physical peak in my twenties, I would have been nowhere near as fit as Dad was when he undertook this journey, given his training and what he had been through by this stage of Galia.
5. I had had a hip replacement just nine months before and had done virtually no exercise in two years because of my condition.
6. I was doing this for 'fun' whereas Dad's life was at stake and he had thousands of enemy soldiers searching for him and every reason in the world to complete the journey as fast as possible.

If this part of this story were a work of fiction, no doubt, I would describe in detail how, heroically and emulating my father's memory, I overcame any physical shortcomings, strived manfully through the high mountain peaks, risking life and limb, but ultimately survived to finish up triumphantly in Seravezza four days later, with the blisters and bruises to prove it.

The real story turned out somewhat differently.

In addition to me and Brian Lett, our party numbered five in total comprising: Tom and Rosemarie MacIntyre, a Canadian husband and wife team who were both extremely fit and very experienced walkers, whom I had met on last year's freedom trail, and Paula, who worked in the British Consul's office in Florence and who had been a Dartmoor Ranger. Our party was to be led by two experienced Italian mountain guides.

We met up on Sunday 16th September 2007 at the Centro in Chiesa di Rossano, the gathering point for all those who were to attempt the war-time escape trail known then as the 'ferrovia'.

I was glad to hear we were to have a roof over our heads each night, as we were to stay in the various mountain refuges provided for these purposes by the Italian national park authority. The downside was that we would have to carry our sleeping bags, mats, spare clothes, food, water and other essentials with us on the trek. As I looked at the bags and equipment my fellow walkers had brought with them it began to dawn on me how woefully unprepared I was.

Paula, Brian and the Canadians had what looked like small bunga-lows strapped to their backs filled with equipment and clothing for every sort of weather imaginable. I, thoughtfully, had brought a 'Kag-in-a-Bag' in case of rain, a fleece in case it got chilly and a small rucksack which doubled as the bag I usually carried my PC to work in at home. It seemed I had taken Brian's advice to 'travel light' a little too literally.

Once on the mountain ranges, due to their inaccessibility by road, there would be no way off other than to make it to the finish line by foot, except (and I loved this word) 'perhaps' by helicopter in an emergency. So there would be a point at which we would each have to make a decision as to whether to commit to fulfilling the whole journey or else decide to turn back whilst we were still within range of more convenient modes of transport.

The next morning, at the Centro, Brian woke his intrepid band of walkers by playing a CD of reveille at full blast an hour before dawn. Reveille was followed by a medley of Queen's greatest hits whilst we swiftly consumed breakfast – 'We are the champions', 'I want to break free' and the curiously prophetic 'Another one bites the dust' and 'I want to ride my bicycle.'

With our collective resolve suitably fired, we set off through the still-sleeping village of Chiesa as the cocks began to crow, heralding the now fast-approaching dawn.

We strolled down through the villages of Paretola and Valle towards the lower reaches of the valley before commencing our climb up to the Alta Via, along which Napoleon had once marched his army to invade Italy. Brian was our guide for the initial section of the trail. He said he would lead us the easiest of the several routes up to the ridge. He set, what for me, seemed like a cracking pace.

The trails were hard under foot and the gradients steep but the views were spectacular. I was really enjoying the walk but even at this early stage I remember thinking that if this was the easy route, all didn't bode well. Our climb took us longer than Brian had hoped, and we eventually reached the ridge of the Alta Via at about 9.20 am. Here we turned south along the Alta Via over Monte Fiorito (Flower Mountain) towards the Magra river. We were to follow the Alta Via for much of the rest of the day. As we reached this spot it began to rain heavily and a very cold wind swept over the high ridge, making me shiver as we paused to get our breath.

My fellow walkers searched their back-strapped-bungalows and duly pulled on their waterproof Bergen jackets and leggings. I made full use of my fleece and Kag-in-the-Bag.

The views from here would have been magnificent, but for the low cloud which now obscured much of the mountain slopes. We were due to meet our guide, Emmanuele, at Casoni at 10.00 am but even at the pace Brian was setting for us were already forty minutes late. Emmanuele allowed us a quick coffee at the hunting lodge at Casoni. Already, my feet were sore from blisters which had begun to form due to the hard surfaces we had been walking across. It was not a good sign. I recalled my Dad telling me as a boy, when I helped him on his milk-round and had suffered from the same ailment, what the SAS's somewhat unconventional 'cure' for blisters had been. Since I didn't think my fellow walkers in more civilised times, would be too keen if I were to start 'weeing' on my feet, I decided to put up with the discomfort.

We started off on the long haul which would eventually take us into the regional town of Aulla. We left at 11.00 am, for what Emmanuele estimated would be a six-hour hike. He was aiming for us to be at Aulla by 17.00, and at Vecchietto before 19.00 hrs. Daylight would begin to fade soon afterwards and he reckoned it would be dark before 20.00 hrs.

As the hours went by, our pace slowed further. By 15.00 Paula was in considerable discomfort from an old hip injury. Emmanuele (who was very slightly built) manfully took Paula's 'Bungalow' from her and carried it, along with his own pack for the rest of the day, with apparent ease. I was also suffering increasing discomfort, not from my new hip but from blisters.

All along the route we came across poignant reminders of the savage guerilla war which had raged here during the dying days of the Third Reich. In one serene spot we found a memorial to six partisans who had together been dispatched in a shady glade, far from any potential witnesses. Was this simply a place of execution? Had these partisans been engaged on a mission and were killed in battle? Were they ambushed or betrayed? Were they hostages or reprisal victims?

In another equally picturesque spot, high on a mountain ridge, two more partisans, who from their birth dates would have both been in their late thirties when killed, were commemorated. The date of their demise caught my eye, the 19th February 1945 – a few days after Dad and his pals had managed to escape and cross to the Allied lines. Who were these men? Had they been anything to do with Galia? Could they have been guides who had helped the SAS to navigate the freedom trail and who had then been captured and killed on their way back?

Meanwhile, it was clear our guide was becoming ever more concerned at our lack of progress. By the time we crawled into Aulla it was 18.15. After twelve hours hiking up and across the mountain trails and after walking around 25 miles I was completely exhausted and extremely grateful to find a decision had been taken to stop at Aulla overnight in the only hotel. Later in my room, when I took my boots off, I didn't recognise my own feet. They were in a terrible state and looked like I had tap-danced on a bacon slicer. I wasn't the only 'casualty'. At breakfast the following morning Paula, too, decided she had met her 'Waterloo'. The final nail in the coffin of my expedition aspirations was the fact that the weather forecast was atrocious, with heavy rain and strong winds sweeping across the region.

I had only managed to reach the foothills of the vast mountain range of Carrara. Bitterly disappointed that I had come all this way to withdraw after only a full day's hiking, I nevertheless took the only decision I could conceivably make in the circumstances. Paula and I made plans to travel back to Pontremoli by train from Aulla in the morning, rather than continue and become a burden on the others.

Brian consoled me by coming up with a new plan to the effect that after a day or two's rest and recovery I could join up with the party again at Vinca, a small town on the route which was the only place on the trail I would be able to access by car. At least I would then get to walk the final forty miles or so of the remaining trail, to what had been the Allied lines near Seravezza, Dad's point of salvation.

After returning to the Centro and resting up for a day, I duly drove to Vinca fully expecting to rejoin the three remaining participants (Brian and the Canadians) to walk the rest of the route. Communications with Brian by mobile phone in such mountainous terrain, though, proved challenging – almost as frustrating as wireless communications must have been for the Galia Squadron. Unfortunately, unbeknown to me, the guides had advised Brian's group to cut Vinca out of their itinerary and to cross over the mountains above it. Due to the distance remaining, the only way they could reach Monte Altissimo, and the ridge that would eventually lead them down through the Gothic Line to Seravezza in the time available was to by-pass the only town en route which was accessible to me. Sadly, I had to accept that my further participation in the walk this year was over.

My trip to Vinca, though, turned out to be a very sobering experience.

Vinca is a stunningly attractive but very isolated market town built into the slopes of the mountains at the end of a valley. There is only one road which leads into and out of the town. On my visit, the sun shone brightly, there was hardly a soul to be found on the streets and all seemed at peace and as it should be in such a place. However, I knew from reading Brian Lett's excellent briefing notes about Vinca that in the summer of 1944 a catastrophe occurred here.

In May 1944 the German forces were finally pushed back from Monte Cassino and the Gustav Line defensive positions in the south. Fighting a fierce rear-guard action they consolidated on a new defensive position – the Gothic Line – south of La Spezia. Over the summer of 1944 the German forces and their Italian fascist *Brigata Nera* allies attempted to suppress all partisan activity in the area. They did so with uncompromising brutality. The massacre of civilians became commonplace as a lesson to others of what would happen if aid was given to the Allies. Vinca was suspected by the Nazis (rightly as it turned out) of being a focal point for partisan activity and as a staging post for escaping POWs.

On the 24th August1944 several trucks full of German SS and Appuanian *Brigata Nera* made their way up the long, winding road into the village. Nearly all the young men of the town were hiding in the mountains to avoid being conscripted into the German Army or becoming slave labourers for the Third Reich. The occupants of the town that day comprised women, children and the elderly.

What followed was later described as a 'barrel organ' of death.[2] The entire population of 174, including 144 women and children, were systematically massacred. No-one was spared, not even the young village priest, Don Luigi Janni, who, hearing of what was happening, hurried back to his flock, only himself to fall victim. When the enemy finally exited the town they left behind piles of bodies. In one spot 29 women were heaped together. One was beheaded, many were naked or half-dressed and some still had their babes-in-arms.

Further atrocities were committed by the perpetrators when they returned the next day to mutilate many of the bodies and to set other villages in the region aflame.

Despite the tragedy inflicted on the innocents here, the survivors in the area continued to give aid, shelter and support to the Allies and any escaping POWs at great risk to themselves. Indeed, the men of SAS Operation Galia passed through Vinca on their long, arduous journey back to the Allied lines in February 1945 and were made welcome and given shelter and food before continuing their journey.

I made my way to the cemetery at the top of the mountain on which the village is perched. The cemetery is dominated by a beautiful marble sarcophagus upon which a sculpture of a young woman is portrayed lying on her back protectively cradling her baby. A wall plaque lists the names of the victims, all, of course, killed on the same day. Many sections of the list had the same surname. One section, with eleven identical surnames, paid silent testament to the fact that babies, toddlers, teenagers, old men, and women of all ages had been slaughtered from that one family. Anyone found in or near the village met the same grisly fate. The local church displayed a special tribute to the heroic young priest Don Luigi Janni.

I remembered an account of Galia provided by Captain Walker Brown that I had read. In it, the SAS Galia commander describes similar atrocities that had occurred at the height of the Rossano *rastrellamento*:

The situation was very dangerous. The sound of automatic gunfire could be heard everywhere and columns of smoke could be seen coming from burning villages. Any village suspected of harbouring SAS or partisans was destroyed. Suspected partisans were shot out of hand.

I saw some 20 young men and girls who had been machine gunned to death against a cemetery wall and six elderly citizens who had been strung up by piano wire.

As I walked around the graveyard at Vinca my journey in Dad's wartime footsteps had, not for the first time, become an incredibly moving experience. Here, in Vinca, was the reality of Dad's war. The reality that he had never been able or willing to convey to me in his lifetime. A brutal, terrible, increasingly desperate struggle for survival against an enemy that had shown itself capable of such heinous crimes against humanity. SAS Operation Galia was, on the one hand, an amazing adventure story of inspirational leadership, incredible hardship, endurance and bravery, whilst on the other it has been rarely mentioned in the history books, a fact that speaks volumes for the modesty and humility of those who took part.

As for my father, for me he saved the best until last. His enduring legacy was to set me a life challenge when I needed it most – to find out what he did. The outcome is that my father has been brought closer to me and in some way 'reborn' in my mind – a vigorous, adventurous yet principled young man, doing a hard, dangerous job in atrocious conditions – doing his duty. Not boasting or glorifying what he had done but quietly getting on with his life after the war, making his family the centre of his world and working to provide for their future – a future he fought so hard to secure.

What a role model for me and my children – his grandchildren to follow.

Thanks Dad.

---

2   Piero Calamandrei, an academic, in a speech delivered in 1954.

A view across the daunting Marble Mountains of Cararra – the escape route for Operation Galia and a 'bridge too far' for the author.

*The memorial to the people of Rossano, the Allied soldiers and airmen
they helped to freedom along the escape trails and the men of SAS
Operation Galia and SAS Operation Blimey. On the reverse the
memorial also pays tribute to Major Gordon Lett.*

The memorial at Parma to the partisans and the fallen (note bound, prone sculpture in the background).

Visiting Sero with the partisan veterans.

Relics of the war – a revolver liberated from the local partisans
a live round from a Vickers machine gun, a set of German Army issue
field glasses and most poignant of all for the author – one army issue
hob-nailed boot complete with parachute chord laces.

Rob Hann and his two sons William (right) and Joseph (left) lead the way along a mountain track towards the village of Sero. Brian Lett carries the banner of the Battaglione Internazionale in honour of his father, SOE Operative Gordon Lett, who founded the battalion.

Left to right: Brian Lett, Serina Deluchi, Rob Hann, Giovani Tongnatelli (the miller), and Antonio Deluchi with the Rossano valley as a backdrop.

The victims of the massacre at Vinca. Note the lists of the same name indicating whole families were murdered.

PART THREE

Roll Call 2013

Opposite

*The whole Galia Squadron posing in front of one of the Dakotas
which dropped them into Rossano on the 27th December 1944.*

*Back row (left to right): Lieut. Edward 'Tinkler' Gibbon, Lance Cpl.
Larley, Pct. 'Spud' Taylor, unidentified, Pct. Matthews?, unidentified,
Pct. Whittaker, Pct. Mulvey, Lieut. James Riccomini, Sgt. Rookes,
Pct. Jimmy Church, Pct. Terry Gargan?, Pct. Eric 'Lofty' Kennedy,
Cpl. Cunningham, Pct Lofty Rose, Lieut. Tom Shaughnessy, Capt. Bob
Walker Brown. Middle row (left to right):
Sgt. Chalky Wright, unidentified, Sgt. Trevor Harrold, unidentified,
Lance Cpl. 'Smokey' Liddington, Pct. Ted Robinson, Pct. Don
Hempstead, unidentified. Front row (left to right): unidentified,
Pct. Pat Duggan, Lance Cpl. Ford?, Cpl. Johnie Johnson, Pct Donnie,
Pct. Harry 'Jock' Shanley, Pct. Stanley 'Spam' Hann,
Pct. Reg Everett.*

*Following input from the SAS association and SAS veterans including
Ted Robinson and after careful scrutiny of all available evidence, for
the first time in 65 years (to the best of our knowledge) we have
managed to put names to the majority of the Galia squad as depicted
above. We have put a question mark where the identification is
tentative. The men we couldn't identify on the photo are: Pct. Sumptor,
Pct. Hildage, Pct. Tate, Cpl. Benson, Pct. Phillips and Pct. Mitchell.*

Dakota 47s

The Galia squad were entirely dependant on air drops for their supplies during the operation. The American Airforce pilots braved the extreme conditions to maintain the men in the field at great personal risk. It therefore seems appropriate to start the roll call with a description of the Dakotas which played such a crucial role in the success of Galia.

DC 47s were the USAAF workhorses and the cargo-hold could be configured for different types of payload. Their main use was, as per Galia, to carry airborne troops, their equipment and supplies into battle. The men generally preferred the American transporters to the Whitley bombers and Albermarles they had trained in. The Whitley was christened 'the flying coffin' by the SAS rank and file. At least with the DC 47 the men could jump out of the aircraft via a doorway whereas on the Whitley they had to drop through a hole in the floor of the aircraft – not an easy feat for a fully equipped paratrooper.

On the DC 47, folding metal or bucket seats could accommodate up to 28 fully-armed paratroops as compared to the Whitley, the maximum load for which was 10. The first major use of the Dakota for transporting airborne troops came in the invasion of Sicily in July 1943 when DC 47s dropped something approaching 4,000 paratroops. They also made a huge contribution to the D-Day landings in June 1944 when in less than 60 hours DC 47s alone airlifted more than 60,000 paratroops and their equipment into Normandy, helping to secure this first vital foothold in France to spearhead the subsequent invasion.[1]

However, these aircraft, whilst functional, were certainly not built for passenger comfort. The smell, the noise and throb of the engines, the lack of any sort of heating, the hard, cold metal seats and the length of the journey – all contributed in a perverse way to whipping up enthusiasm of those inside to make the leap 'into the unknown' once the green light appeared.

---

1   From *The Concise Guide to American Aircraft of WW2* by David Mondey, 1996, Smithmark Publishers.

Many of the Galia squad, having been in their early or mid twenties at the time of Operation Galia, have now passed away, including, since the first edition of this book, Pct Ted Robinson.

However, several family members of the Galia squad have now been in touch, thanks to the wonders of the internet. The SAS Operation Galia 'extended family' is firmly established. Some have kindly agreed to share what they know or were told about Operation Galia by their Galia connected relatives. I am extremely grateful to all who have felt able to contribute memories and recollections. If other Galia family members make themselves known in future I hope to add pages to the E-version of this book and to include similar biographies in later hard copy re-issues.

I have commenced the Roll Call with the obituary (and related correspondence) of the commanding officer of Operation Galia, Lieutenant Colonel Bob Walker Brown (or Captain Walker Brown as he was then).

Brian Lett's subsequent researches as recorded in his excellent book SAS in Tuscany add to the current knowledge about those involved in SAS Operation Galia and I have included some information here which was not known on the first edition of this book in tribute to those men.

Rob Hann, 2013

Lieutenant Colonel Bob Walker Brown – CO of SAS Operation Galia

Lieutenant Colonel Bob Walker Brown DSO, the inspirational commanding officer of SAS Operation Galia, sadly passed away three months before the publication of this book, aged 90. Although I never got the opportunity to meet him, at least I did speak to Colonel Bob on one memorable occasion by telephone as noted in the epilogue above. I hope this book will stand as a fitting tribute to a truly extraordinary man.

The Daily Telegraph published a full obituary on the 18th September 2009. The obituary contained a summary of Galia and outlined the main highlights of Walker Brown's service record, including an account of his escape from captivity in 1943. Unfortunately, it also contained a potentially misleading statement regarding the circumstances in which the partisan 'Chella' met his fate, which Brian Lett was quick to spot and correct. A copy of Brian's letter to the *Telegraph* is also reproduced below in the interests of historical accuracy.

Lieutenant-Colonel Bob Walker Brown

Lieutenant-Colonel Bob Walker Brown, who has died aged 90, was awarded the DSO in 1945 for leading a highly successful guerrilla raid by the SAS in Italy.

On December 27 1944 Walker Brown, then a captain in the 2nd Special Air Service Regiment (2 SAS), and 32 all ranks were dropped by parachute behind the enemy lines in the Apennines, north of La Spezia.

SAS operations were carried out in the knowledge that Hitler had issued an order that all enemy commandos, parachutists and other special units captured away from the immediate battle zone were to be shot at once. Any German officer who failed to comply was himself to be shot.

The operation was codenamed 'Galia'. Flying conditions were dreadful, and the leading aircraft, in heavy cloud, flew straight into a mountainside. During his own descent, Walker Brown's leg bag broke free at 400ft, smashing his carbine.

Although handicapped by deep snow, rugged terrain and primitive radio communications, he led his men over the mountains, fording hazardous, fast-flowing rivers, attacking transport columns, mortaring enemy-held villages, mining roads and ambushing infantry. The Germans were forced to deploy 6,000 troops in a drive to eliminate him.

Some partisans were reliable, despite savage reprisals by the Germans. Others could not be trusted and were not above sending false ground signals in order to steal supplies dropped by air. One guide was summarily shot after he led an SAS patrol into a trap.

The nights were bitterly cold, and goat tracks were covered in ice and impossible to use. On one occasion, Walker Brown and his men struggled up a mountain 7,000ft high after a forced march of 57 hours.

A German captain, found dallying with an Italian girl, was captured. With Walker Brown's pistol at his back, he was forced to lead the way across the Gothic Line at night using old shepherds' paths. Two enemy patrols were encountered but their forced 'escort' got them through undiscovered.

Walker Brown dodged the dragnet and personally accounted for many of the substantial casualties inflicted on the Germans. The citation for his DSO paid tribute to his 'unparalleled guerrilla skill and personal courage' in keeping his force intact in a two-month mountain campaign in the depths of winter. His fellow troop commander in Italy was captured with his signaller. Both were shot.

Robert Walker Brown, the son of a Scottish surgeon, was born at Sutton Coldfield on April 9 1919 and educated privately.

At the outbreak of war he was mobilised with the Royal Engineer TA Reserve before transferring to the Highland Light Infantry (HLI) and joining the 2nd Battalion in Egypt in 1941.

He was wounded during the Battle of the Cauldron in the Western Desert in June 1942 and was captured by the Germans.

After three months in a POW hospital at Lucca he was transferred to Campo Prigioneri di Guerra 21 at Chieti in the foothills of the Apennines, north-east of Rome.

The Italian guards were alert; there were microphones in the cells, and three attempts to build escape tunnels were discovered early in 1943. An Italian officer confided that a successful attempt would result in the camp commandant's departure to the Russian front and that the guards would not hesitate to lob grenades down any hole they discovered.

The blocks were surrounded by flagstone and cement paving leading to an 18ft perimeter wall with sentries, searchlights and trip wires. Cautious investigation by Walker Brown and his comrades revealed a lifting ring giving access to a storm drain sump which led to a brick chamber about 4ft deep and 15 inches square. It was close to the perimeter track that was patrolled by armed *Carabinieri*.

A very small officer was equipped with a poker and inserted, despite his protestations, into the sump with instructions to remove enough of the bricks to open up a larger chamber. Contact was maintained by a code of taps on the sump lid and a rota of POW sentries was organised to give warning of the approach of a patrol.

Shift work was established and two, and later three, tunnellers went down after the morning muster parade. Spoil was rolled into balls and packed into the walls of the ablutions hut. A prismatic compass that had escaped several searches was used to keep the direction of the tunnel on the correct bearing.

The guards were becoming increasingly suspicious. Snap searches slowed the work but, after three weeks, 20ft of tunnel had been dug. Of a camp complement of some 900 officers, fewer than 40 were engaged in escape attempts; and the sight of naked, clay-covered men jumping through the windows of the ablutions hut caused resentment among those who saw these activities as a threat to a peaceful life.

After five weeks, the end of the tunnel was close to the wall and a deep level chamber had to be dug to get under the foundations. After further digging, the tunnellers struck a main sewer.

This had to be opened up to help dispose of the soil, but the air was so foul that there were several cases of fainting, and an improvised oil lamp flickered out after 20 minutes. For some time, all work was carried out in complete darkness until an air pipe had been made from Red Cross food tins, sealed with clay and completed with an air pump fashioned from a tin and an old boot.

When the guards found escape rations and home-made compasses, more snap searches were introduced. By this time, six men were in the tunnel. Six non-digging officers pretended to be ill in bed and their names were handed to the Italians each day on a nominal roll. Dummies were placed in their beds and then paraded to cover the absentees. After four months' digging, the foundations of the wall had been breached and the tunnel measured some 140ft. A breakout chamber was built, but as final escape preparations were being made Italy surrendered, and the camp was taken over by a company of German parachutists.

When their commander ordered an assembly for the immediate evacuation of the camp, Walker Brown and a number of POWs hid in the tunnel and waited underground for several hours before breaking out at night.

With two companions, he headed south and walked for 10 days, moving only at night, fording rivers and dodging enemy patrols. They were recaptured briefly by a section of German infantry but got away when they came under fire and reached the lines of a battalion of the Northamptonshire Regiment and relative safety on October 5 1943.

Appointed MBE for his escape, Walker Brown was posted to an infantry training centre at Aberdeen, but he soon became bored and joined 2 SAS at Prestwick. Sent on a parachute course, he landed on the roof of a double-decker bus full of Wrens on his first jump.

On September 1 1944 he was dropped as 'stick commander' with a troop of armed Jeeps into the Forest of Chatillon, north of Dijon, to reinforce No 1 Squadron, 2nd SAS, commanded by Major Roy Farran.

Over France, they ran into heavy flak and his aircraft was damaged. Running in over the drop zone, one man was killed when his static line parted and Walker Brown, who jumped next, was relieved to see his canopy open.

With their machine guns, Brens and mortars, they were a formidable force and took part in an attack on the German garrison which occupied the chateau at Chaumont.

Walker Brown wrote afterwards: 'Tracer, ball and armour-piercing shells were flying all over the place. German rein-forcements soon appeared, so we pulled out leaving brewed-up vehicles, smouldering fires and, according to the French, 110 casualties. We lost one killed and two wounded.' The forest cover, country roads and tracks were used to launch a series of ambushes before the party returned to England later in the month.

After the war Walker Brown rejoined the HLI but subsequently served with 21 SAS as training major and 22 SAS as second-in-command before commanding 23 SAS. He then served with the Defence Intelligence Staff before retiring from the army in 1964.

His many friends delighted in his political incorrectness, occasional cussedness, intolerance of idleness and mischievous sense of humour. He was grappling with new languages, digital photography and the intricacies of computer science at an age when many would opt for a less exacting life. Settled in Wiltshire, he was a keen angler and fished the Avon and the Wylye.

Bob Walker Brown died on August 16. He married first, in 1955, Leonie Hossack. She predeceased him. He married secondly, in 1996, Helen Leeming, who survives him. There were no children.

Dear Sir,

I have read with interest today the obituary of Lieut. Colonel Bob Walker Brown, a lifetime friend of my father's, and latterly a valued friend of mine. Bob Walker Brown was an exceptional man, as the obituary properly reflects. However, the obituary contains one error which I believe that Lieut. Colonel Walker Brown and others under his command would have wished me to correct. Paragraph 6 of the obituary reads: 'Some partisans were reliable despite savage reprisals by the Germans. Others could not be trusted and were not above sending false ground signals in order to steal supplies dropped by air. One guide was summarily shot after he led an SAS patrol into a trap.'

The clear suggestion, or inference to be drawn, from the last sentence of that paragraph is that a partisan guide betrayed the SAS stick, and was shot by them. Neither is true. The safe arrival of Walker Brown and his men at DZ Huntsville on the 27th December 1944 was mainly due to the fact that partisans under the command of my father, Major Gordon Lett DSO, and other partisans leaders, had sealed the valley of Rossa no so that no enemy troops could interfere with the landing. Thereafter, guides from my father's International Battalion of partisans acted as guides for the SAS.

The guide involved in the incident mentioned was a young man called Chella Leonardo di Chella Narcisso, from the village of Valeriano near La Spezia. He was one of three young cousins from that village who had joined my father's partisans. Two of the three cousins were captured and murdered during Operation Galia by enemy forces because of the help that they gave to the SAS.

The SAS stick for which Chella Leonardo was the guide sheltered overnight in a hut on the edge of a small village called Montebello. They were betrayed by one of the villagers to the fascist *Brigata Nera*. The *Brigata Nera* surrounded the hut, and took the SAS and Chella Leonardo prisoner. Chella was tortured by the *Brigata Nera*, and then executed by them. The fate of the SAS was far better – they were taken prisoner and survived the war.

The accuracy of the above account is attested to in the records of No 1 Special Force, held at the National Archives in Kew. The Commander of Special Force, Florence, at the relevant time was a Major Charles Macintosh. My father's report to Major

Macintosh of this incident was as follows:

'Please could you do all possible to obtain an award for the following person: Chella Leonardo di Chella Narcisso: This was my lad who was with the SAS stick. On being captured, he was tortured, refused to talk, and was then shot. Something will also have to be done about a pension for his family.'

Lieut. Col. Walker Brown himself wrote in his debrief report following successful ex-filtration from Operation Galia: 'Lieutenant Shaughnessy and the whole of his stick reported captured in Montebello by a party of *Brigata Nera* who were said to be dressed in civilian clothes. The Italian guide was interrogated, tortured and then shot by the *Brigata Nera*.'

Thus it is clear that Chella Leonardo, and indeed the other guides used by Operation Galia, were to be regarded as heroes not villains. It is certainly true that some rival bands of partisans [not under my father's command] attempted by various means to pinch the stores intended for Operation Galia. However, any suggestion that the men of SAS Operation Galia were betrayed by partisans of the Battaglione Internazionale of Rossano is quite untrue. The opposite is the case. Chella Leonardo is still honoured in his own community as a courageous young man, and a small British contingent regularly lays a wreath on the spot where he was murdered.

Yours faithfully,

Brian Gordon Lett QC

Lieutenant James Arthur Riccomini and SAS Operation Tombola

James Riccomini was raised and educated in Nottingham, at the Henry Mellish Grammar School, before making his home in Kent prior to the outbreak of World War Two.

Lieutenant James Riccomini was already a decorated war hero before taking part in SAS Operation Galia. Riccomini had been taken prisoner by the Germans in June 1941, and had ultimately wound up at Gavi, a medieval fortress in Liguria used as a punishment camp for persistent escapers and prominent prisoners, who included the 'Phantom Major' himself – Colonel David Stirling, founder of the SAS. Like his two senior officers on Galia (Captain Walker Brown and Major Lett), Riccomini managed to escape following the Italian armistice in 1943. After many adventures and narrow escapes working with Italian partisans behind the lines, Riccomini carried out several engagements against enemy forces and finally made his 'home run' via Switzerland on the 11th January 1944.

He was awarded the MBE for these daring escapades and for his work behind the lines.

After a short period of recuperation, Riccomini joined 2nd SAS Regiment but apparently did not have time to undergo formal parachute training before being selected for Galia. Riccomini's value to the operation as an Italian speaker, experienced at working with the partisans, was obvious. He was brought along as interpreter and partisan liaison officer. Any parachute training shortcomings were overlooked in the interests of expediency.

Accordingly, Riccomini's first parachute jump took place on the 27th December 1944 into enemy territory, as second in command to Captain Walker Brown's 3 Troop, B Squadron, 2nd SAS on Operation Gallia. At some stage during the operation, Riccomini's injured an ankle after a bad fall. This injury caused him considerable difficulties during an Operation which relied on fitness, stamina, mobility and speed to engage and avoid the enemy.

Despite his injury and the appalling conditions faced by the men, Riccomini acquitted himself in the finest traditions of the SAS. Captain Walker Brown, who by all accounts, was not one for handing out gratuitous compliments, regarded Riccomini's actions as deserving of formal recognition and duly recommended him for the Military Cross. The London Gazette of the 1st March 1945 records Riccomini's MC citation as follows:

Lieutenant James Arthur Riccomini MBE. M.C. Army Air Corps, 'For gallant and distinguished services in Italy'.

'This officer dropped behind enemy lines by parachute on the 27th December, 1944, as 2nd in command of an SAS troop. On the 11th January, 1945, he was commanding a detachment which ambushed a German column on the Genoa–Spezia road near Bocca del Pignone. One lorry was completely destroyed and a staff car was riddled with machine-gun fire. Thirty casualties (killed or wounded) were inflicted on the Germans. The success of this operation was entirely due to this officer's personal skill and courage. He directed the attack on the column in full view of the enemy, completely ignoring the fire returned by them.

On the 19th January, 1945, he again ambushed two vehicles on the Pontremoli-La Spezia main road as they were crossing a bridge. One truck was destroyed and a number of casualties were inflicted on the Germans.

When 6,000 enemy troops were conducting a Rastrellamento against the SAS contingent on several occasions it was entirely this officer's skill and personal courage which prevented the enemy from capturing or killing personnel under his command. Despite a badly poisoned foot, in Arctic conditions of gales, sleet and snow, he made his way through deep snow drifts with his men, never failing to carry out any task allotted him. Throughout the operations lasting from 27th December, 1944, to 20th February, 1945, he was a personal source of inspiration and encouragement to his men. His conduct could not have been excelled in any way being far above the normal call of duty.'

Riccomini's achievements were all the more remarkable given at one stage he was considered to be so badly injured that he was ordered by the medical officer (Captain Milne) to remain behind the lines until he had fully recovered, rather than attempt to exfiltrate with the remainder of the troop. However, in the event, Riccomini managed to recover sufficiently to lead the second group of SAS troops out of the Rossano valley and along the dangerous escape route towards the American forward positions past the heavily defended Gothic Line. On 15th February 1945, Riccomini and his men, following Walker Brown's troop, successfully exfiltrated back into the Allied lines.

But Riccomini's war did not end there.

In his book Stirling's Men (which chronicles some of the first-hand memoires of wartime SAS 'Originals') Gavin Mortimer records that despite his many daring escapades, Riccomini yearned for the war to be over so that he could at last return to the wife he had married in September 1939. In a poignant letter to her he wrote "The real thing that worries me is that I might not ever be able to settle down after all this . . . however, darling remember, that I do think of you very often and that one day I will be home again.'

Before he could honour his promise to his wife, Riccomini had one more battle to fight. Towards the end of February 1945, Major Roy Farran, CO of 2 SAS, 3 Squadron was directed to send an SAS team into Reggio Province to join up with a partisan battalion to harass German communications in the event of a proposed offensive by the American 15th Army Group. Riccomini was selected for the operation, codenamed 'Tombola'.

Among the participants taking part in Tombola were two other Galia 'veterans', Sergeant Sid Guscott who joined the Galia squad during the Operation by trecking across the mountains through enemy territory with two other comrades – known as Operation Brake 2 and a newly recruited partisan volunteer, a certain Louis 'Pippo' Siboldi who had returned with Walker Brown having helped to navigate the Galia troop over the Marble Mountains to safety.

On the 10th March 1945 Riccomini launched himself for only the second time, along with a 40 odd SAS comrades and Pippo Siboldi, into enemy territory in Northern Italy. Tombola was led by Major Farran who, although he had been ordered not to go on the operation himself, claimed to have tripped and fallen out of the aeroplane. Fortunately for Farran, he happened to be wearing a parachute at the time.

The chosen attacking force was divided into Farran's headquarters stick and three columns; left, right and centre. Riccomini's task was to lead the assault on a German Generals' billet by the centre column which comprised nine British other ranks and nineteen Russians and Italian partisans under Captain Mike Lees.

On 26th March Farran's force set out towards a rendezvous on the edge of the target area which was reached unobserved at 02.00 hrs on the 27th. Riccomini's column moved off and covered the two hundred or so yards to his target, the Villa Rossi, which contained the German Corps commander, a visiting divisional General and thirty-seven officers and a significant contingent of other troops. Another group swept right to form a defensive ring on the flank and the left column moved off to attack another target, the Villa Calvi, which was nearby.

But before Riccomini's column could reach the Villa Rossi, the attack on the Villa Calvi began. With the German defences now fully on alert and with Major Farran's piper playing Highland Laddie in the background – '. . .just to let the Germans know they had the British to contend with' – Riccomini went into action.

Farran's report of the action records that Riccomini '. . . killed four sentries through the iron railing with his tommy-gun and then rushed the door. It was open, but a hail of fire came from within. After fierce fighting, the ground floor was taken, but the Germans resisted furiously from the upper floors, firing and throwing grenades down a spiral staircase. Captain Mike Lees led one attack up the stairs which was repulsed with heavy casualties. Lieutenant Riccomini led another attack which was similarly repulsed.'

After twenty minutes the raiding party withdrew but Lieutenant Riccomini along with his Galia comrade, Sergeant Guscott and Corporal Bolden were not among their number.

Lieutenant James Arthur Riccomini MBE, MC was just 27 when he was killed on the 23rd March 1945, only six weeks before the end of the war, by a hail of machine-gun bullets leading his men into battle one final time. He is buried in a war cemetery in Milan.

In Albinea, Northern Italy in 1985 a square was renamed 'Piazza Caduti Alleati di Ville Rossi' (Square of the Fallen Allies of Villa Rossi) in tribute.

Major Roy Farran, though considered for court martial for disobeying orders and for jumping from the plane to take part in Tombola, was later awarded the Military Cross.

Such are the fortunes of war.

The American USAAF Colonel

The support provided both in terms of the original drop behind enemy lines on the 27th January 1944 and the subsequent supply drops to the Galia Squad in the field by the US Airforce was significant and essential to the success of the mission. Regular supplies of food, ammunition, weapons and equipment had to be accurately dropped in by parachute at great personal risk to the (mainly) American pilots and air crew.

One Pilot in particular, stood out in his willingness to put his life at risk to help maintain the troops on the ground by flying supply drops during the harshest of conditions.

Major Roy Farran, CO of 3 Squadron 2SAS , in his book of his wartime exploits, paid fulsome tribute to the bravery of this pilot who was destined to help Farran himself on a subsequent SAS Operation (Tombola) in Italy:

"I felt a surge of gratitude to the American Squadron Leader, the lean colonel who had commanded the Dakotas from Leghorn, for he had already done so much for us. I remember how when Walker Brown's men were scattered by the Germans in the mountains north of La Spezia and were sick to death with dysentery and scabies he personally flew in Jock Milnes our doctor through fog clouded mountains in a lone unarmed Dakota dropping him accurately in an isolated valley".

Thanks to intensive research by Brian Lett (see SAS in Tuscany), it is now possible to put a name to the brave air force colonel who risked so much in support of his British allies on both Operation Galia and Operation Tombola:

Colonel John Cerny, a much decorated American veteran

Brian Lett has also managed to identify the names of the
seven air crew who were tragically killed on the 30th
December 1944 attempting to re-supply the Galia Squad
who were as follows:

* Pilot - First Lieutenant Don Alan Ray of Illinois
* Co-pilot Second Lieutenant Earl.S.Hurlbut also of Illinois
* Staff Sergeant William H Close Jr from Baltimore,
  Maryland
* Staff Sergeant Israel Goodman from New London, Connecticutt
* Staff Sergeant Fred Reyther from Fort Worth, Texas.

Two British casualties completed the ill-fated flight crew

* Corporal William Oldershaw, RASC from Nottingham
* Driver James Wilfred Cox RASC

SAS in Tuscany contains more information about the
circumstances surrounding the accident and other
relevant information. Brian Lett intends to lead a ceremony
in Rossano to dedicate a memorial to the brave airmen who
so tragically perished trying to help re-supply their SAS
comrades during the Galia mission.

PcT Ted Robinson – SAS Operation Galia HQ Stick

Contribution from Alan Robinson, son of Ted Robinson

My Father, Ted Robinson was fortunate, towards the end of his life, to meet Brian Lett and Rob Hann and get a much fuller picture of what had happened on Operation Galia; in particular he was overjoyed to hear that all 32 of his comrades survived the operation.

Despite the fact he had just turned 21 prior to Galia Ted Robinson had already seen action behind enemy during the D-Day landings on SAS Operation Rupert.

On Galia, Ted, was one of the wireless operators, As one of the youngest members of the squad, he was ordered to stick closely to Walker Brown and the HQ stick. Accordingly, he was among the SAS faction who made the marathon 59 hour forced march to Buzzo in the North to escape the enemy dragnet. Ted was able to provide many more details about the Galia raid from his direct involvement in the actions described in this book,

He recalled the old man collecting wood for the village oven where once a week the wives brought their chestnut loaves for baking. The simple circular stone huts where animals and farmers lived and the chestnuts were dried, and the open pasture land which has now been replaced by forests.

Sometimes there were memories of his SAS chums, such as Stanley 'Spam' Hann who accompanied him to a chemist shop in Leghorn to process their photographs of the Galia Operation; Ted Gargan, the "Boy Bandit" always festooned with guns and ammunition; "Sir John" Matthews who often mimicked the posh accent of the officers to the amusement of the troop; and Captain Walker-Brown who retained his formality while fostering a sense of team spirit and friendliness among the group. Above all there was Joe Cunningham, the "greatest WT operator", who went with Ted after Galia to the Radio HQ at Florence, where they were greeted like lost brothers by the other wireless operators who had waited for weeks during Galia for a message, fearing that they must have been killed in action.

After demob, Ted started work at "The Plant" locomotive works in Doncaster where he sometimes mentioned to his workmates what he had done in the war. They thought he was making it up, so Ted kept quiet from then on. As his children grew up he made occasional mention of his life and wartime action in Italy, especially his fascination with the near-mediaeval life of the people of Rossano.

My Father, in his own words, provided a message (replicated below) to be included in the original edition of this book.

My father, Ted Robinson passed away on the 10th January 2012 surrounded by his loving family and is greatly missed by all who knew him. His final years though were greatly enriched by the information and engagement with others interested in the Galia story:

Message from Galia wireless operator
Ted Robinson

It has stirred many emotions to reminisce about events all those years ago on Operation Galia. It is difficult to imagine what happened in those ruggedly beautiful hills. Companionship and friendships were forged between the SAS and the true partisans, which was essential to our survival.

I would particularly like to thank the people of the villages of Rossano and Buzzo, and especially the two brave young women of Buzzo who brought cooked food – my first-ever proper minestrone – to our hideaway when the Alpini troops were hot on our heels, moving like strings of pearls through the snowy mountains.

I would also like to make a special mention of my friend Joe Cunningham, the best wireless operator of them all. He and the operators in Florence were the vital link who helped us to continue the operation.

Parachutist Ted Robinson,
Wireless Operator, 3rd Squadron, 2nd SAS

Parachutist Ted Robinson,
Wireless Operator, 3rd Squadron, 2nd SAS

PcT Frank Mulvey - SAS Operation Galia - HQ Stick

Contributed by Tara Mulvey - daughter of Pct Frank Mulvey and the Mulvey family

Francis William Kindlan Mulvey, known as Frank, was born in Dublin and came to England aged approximately 16 to join the army after the war broke out. It is not clear which regiment Frank first joined but he joined 2 SAS, 3rd Squadron in 1944, where he remained until the end of the war.

His time in the SAS was action packed.

It is now known that he took part in Operation Galia but then, in common with many of the other Galia Squadron members and only a month after exfiltrating, he was parachuted back into Northern Italy (Albinea) in March 1945. Frank Mulvey took part in Operation Tombola, one of the SAS's most celebrated missions of WW2. Tombola was the last of these kinds of operations in Northern Italy and the only one that Frank mentioned to his children.

Major Roy Farran and Captain Mike Lees jointly led the operation, with the help of the partisans but Operation Tombola should never have taken place. Allied High Command gave orders calling off the attack shortly before it was due to take place. Against orders, Farran and Lees made the decision to go ahead regardless and attack Villas Rossi and Calvi which were being used as headquarters for the German 51st Mountain Corps.

Major Farran requested that a 'piper' be parachuted in, to pipe the men into Battle and to scare the living daylights out of the enemy. The piper would have also made it clear to the Germans that this was a British operation, the hope being that this might prevent reprisals against the local population at a later date.

Frank used to talk about how the sound of those pipes echoed round the mountains as the men carried out the attack on the two enemy strong-holds. Perhaps not surprisingly, he had a particular fondness for bagpipes for the rest of his life.

The battle and subsequent fire-fight was extremely intense, the Germans resisted fiercely. Three SAS were killed in the attack (Ltn James Riccomini, Sgt Sid Guscott and Corporal Sammy Bolden). Frank was seriously injured having been shot in the right knee.

During the withdrawal, Frank was carried by his comrades to a local farmer and arrangements were made for him to be smuggled through the mountains in a cart to safety. He was hidden in the farmer's hayloft and, because of the severity of his wounds, local priest was called to administer the last rights should it have become necessary.

In later life Frank would occasionally talk about being shot in the knee and carried by the Italian partisans to safety but the full extent of his story only came to light in April 2012, after research via the internet.

Frank's daughters initially discovered photographs on the internet of Frank with the SAS Galia squadron, taken at Brindisi airport just before flying out for Operation Galia (in fact, the photograph on the cover of this book). This led to contact being made with the other Galia relatives and to obtaining the 'SAS Operation Galia' book.

Then came information from Italy. Michele Becchi got in touch to say he had information regarding our father's role on Operation Tombola. After contact was made with Michele, he became very keen for Frank's children to talk to an Italian journalist, Matteo Incerti, who had written a book on Operation Tombola which included a whole chapter on the SAS man who had been shot in the knee and carried to safety.

Matteo confirmed that the casualty was Pct Frank Mulvey from the original diary entry made by the Priest on the night he had attended Frank, where he had written down Frank's name and service number. Matteo also revealed that not only was he still in touch with the two partisans that had saved Frank's life, but they were in fact women. They had been teenagers at the time and did not know whether their patient had survived after he had left their charge.

An emotional re-union took place via Skype between Frank's children, Giovanna Quadreri and Mercedes Zobbi, with Matteo acting as interpreter. Frank's children got to hear first hand what actually had happened to their dad after he was wounded. They also thanked the ladies for saving their dad's life and in turn, the two ladies thanked Frank for 'fighting for their freedom'. They went on to explain in detail how they took Frank from the hayloft, put him in a cart pulled by a donkey and with the help of the farmer, began the 67km journey through the mountains to hand him over to the British for treatment. On route, they were shot at by Germans from the other side of the mountain. The farmer panicked and tipped Frank out of the cart, down the side of the road and ran off taking his cart and mule with him.

Frank was suffering badly but he shouted for the girls to run away. Instead, they hid until the firing stopped, managed to find another mule (courtesy of a different farmer), tied Frank to the mule with rope and continued their journey, attempting to sooth his pain all the way until they reached safety. They eventually handed Frank over to the British and they never saw him again. They said it was wonderful to know that he had survived his ordeal and had gone on to have a family.

Frank's two elder daughters, his son and grandson have since been to Italy to visit Giovanna and Mercedes in person and all five of his children travelled there in March 2013 for the official, annual Operation Tombola Memorial.

After the war and once he had recovered from his wounds, Frank returned to London to try and settle into post war life. He met and then married his wife Katherine Joan Carter in 1961. They moved to Hastings, East Sussex where Frank initially worked as a bus conductor. They had five children and quickly became part of the community where they lived, making many good friends who still to this day speak fondly of them both. Most of them did not know that Frank was in the SAS, right up until he died from cancer in 1982.

Although so much has been revealed, the research continues for Frank and his family who are currently awaiting his military service records, which will hopefully reveal what he was doing for the three years leading up to Operation Galia.

Frank's family would also like to thank all the Galia relatives for their books, information, and photos, without which this journey would never have started.

Pct Pat Duggan – SAS Operation Galia No.3 Stick

Contribution from Sean Duggan – son of Pct Sidney 'Pat' Duggan

Sidney Duggan, always known as Pat, grew up in the East End and was working for the Smithfield and Argentine Meat Company when war broke out. He was already in the Territorial Army and, after finding that the London Irish regiment were already full, volunteered to join the Queen's Regiment when World War two broke out.

Finding himself stuck in an anti-aircraft battalion on the east coast, where "the only excitement was raiding the cookhouse", he volunteered to join the Parachute Regiment.

Pat served in 2 Para in North Africa with the Desert Rats. After that he saw action in Sicily and, after volunteering for the SAS, spent the last six months of the war in 3 Squadron, 2 SAS. This included taking part in Operation Galia, an experience which, although he rarely spoke about his wartime adventures, remained seared in his memory until the end of his life.

On Galia he recalled that during one unforgettable ambush he and a stick comrade were ordered to man a Bren gun beneath a mountain road while the rest of the party took up positions above it. The pair built a sanger out of rocks which provided limited protection.

When a large army convoy came down the road they opened fire. They managed to loose off a couple of rounds from the Bren gun but then it stubbornly jammed. A hail of bullets erupted towards their position, pinging off the rocks all around them as they pressed their bodies into the snow. When the fire fight was over, Pat and his comrade in arms, stood up, unscathed, amazed to be alive.

On Operation Galia, Pat said it was so cold that they had to keep their boots on for days on end because their feet had swollen so much. Had they taken their boots off they would never have been able to get them back on again. Weapons and firing mechanisms were also a problem in the freezing conditions. They had no choice but to urinate on their carbines and bren guns to get them to operate.

During the enemy search and destroy action, Pat and his SAS stick were hunted day and night, up and down the steep, snow covered, mountain ranges. Starved and exhausted, they took temporary refuge in a mountain hut. To Pat it seemed like only minutes after he had fallen asleep that he was being shaken awake by one of his comrades on sentry duty. They could seeshapes in snow camouflage uniform advancing up the slope towards them. The SAS men slipped out of the back of the hut and pressed on up the mountain, through the deep snow, using the thick forest as cover. A few minutes later they watched the hut go up in flames –torched in retaliation by the hunter force sent to kill them.

One evening, at dusk, Pat's stick had to cross a clearing directly beneath a German machine gun post. Despite their lack of camouflaged clothing they got across undetected by rolling across in the snow one at a time right under the noses of their enemy.

Pat said he became so tired from the endless marching through the mountains in deep snow that he longed to just lie down in it for a few minutes to sleep – even though he knew it would mean certain death.

For the remainder of his life, Pat remained deeply grateful to the Italian villagers and partisans who risked their lives to help him by providing food and shelter, some of whom of course, as we now know, paid the ultimate price.

At the end of the war, when the SAS was scheduled for disbandment, he was one of those chosen to go for officer selection with the aim of preserving the skills and ethos of the regiment in the regular army. He hoped the SAS would be reformed one day when circumstances permitted (which of course it was - in 1952).

But, like almost all of those from the SAS put forward, Pat was turned down by the War Office Selection Board, something he attributed to the SAS's unconventional approach to soldiering and prejudice against the SAS from regulars, some of whom dubbed them "canteen cowboys".

Demobbed in 1946, Pat joined the 21st SAS (Artists) along with his beloved younger brother Terry who went on to be among the last intake of officers into the Indian Army. Tragically, Terry was killed in action following an ambush during the Malay Emergency.

Unable to settle back into life in post-war, bombed out London after his many adventures, Pat took a job in Bahrain with the Bahrain Petroleum Company. His agile mind and mathematical ability allowed him to make rapid career progress and he joined Caltex who sent him as commissioning engineer for the rebuilding of the refinery at Bec d'Ambes.

Pat left there in 1950 to head-up the engineering section at Bordeaux for the US Army, responsible for the biggest ammunition dump in Europe, 5 major depots and a port, as well as building the dock at Bassins.

Three years later he joined an independent geophysical engineering company and carried out seismic work in Italian Somaliland and the Gulf, before returning to France to help set up Exploration Geophysique Rogers, operating out of Pau.

There, Pat met his future wife Audrey, on board a transatlantic liner coming back from North America. Romance blossomed after Pat accidently dived on top of her in the swimming pool.

Pat and Audrey married in 1956 and he left the oil business to pursue a long standing interest in antiques - an interest he shared with Audrey whose family had been antique dealers since the 19th century.

For the next decade they dealt in antiques, first in Hastings and then in Tunbridge Wells. Together they had four children and accumulated a wonderful variety of friends. They retired in 1969, but after a brief spell in Worthing moved to Bexhill and went back into business. Pat continued working until a few days before his death of cancer in April 1993.

The intensity and camaraderie that Pat experienced whilst serving in the wartime SAS was something he never forgot. Although he was not one for re-unions, he was very proud to have been part of the regiment and supported its association throughout his life.

Corporal Joe Cunningham Wireless Operator, SAS Operation Galia - HQ Stick

Contribution from John Jelly, Nephew of Cpl Joe Cunningham *(who in turn says he is indebted to Major Oakes' son William who has helped John discover so much information over the last few years about his uncle Joe).*

Corporal William Cunningham, always know as 'Joe' as he disliked his initials ('WC') for obvious reasons, was born in Maltby, Yorkshire on the 11/04/15. He enlisted in the Royal Signals 280 Regiment on 05/01/34 and embarked for India on 20/11/37 where he joined the 4th India Division Signals. He entered Egypt with Force K-4 on 04/10/39, was appointed corporal and was posted to the 10th India Division Signals

In 1942, he was attached in some way with 1 SAS in North Africa, and is mentioned in Malcolm Playdel's book 'Born Of The Desert', this is evidenced by his annotations peppering the margins of the copy I have in my possession. He may have been commanded by the legendary SAS Colonel Paddy Mayne.

1943 was a bad year for Joe. He was badly wounded. From the official records, it reads:

'Fracture to the base of the skull with complete paralysis of the 7th nerve. Serious injury likely to interfere: Decision of competent authority: On duty - not to blame.'
(Bell's Palsy).

Joe's records show he returned from the Middle East to the UK on 03/02/44;

He was then posted to 38th division: Signals 11/02/44 but was then posted to SAS Brigade Signals section on the 17/04/44.

In August & September 1944 Joe was involved in Operation Wallace, under Major Farran, and was partnered by Pct Freddie Oakes. This was a Jeep operation deep behind enemy lines

In late November-December he had brief parachute training in Manchester. SAS Operation Galia, commanded by Captain Bob Walker-Brown, was probably his first operational jump. Here, as we know, he was partnered by his good friend and fellow wireless operator Pct Ted Robinson.

After just a few short weeks after Galia, in March 1945 he was involved in Operation Tombola under Major Farran. He was partnered this time by PcT Green.

Joe Cunningham was awarded the following:
* 1939-45 Star
• France and Germany Star
• Africa Star
• Italy Star • Defence Medal

From 1947 to 1954 he was involved with 21 SAS (reservists) and was discharged in February of that year.

As a civilian he worked for some years at ICI in Middlesbrough. Later, he managed a sweet shop in Thornaby, Stockton-on-Tees. This is the part that I remember best, as we got free sweets and that's how come he became my favourite uncle. Many years after that, I went to Assisi in Italy with him on a pilgrimage, he was always very religious. I asked him about what he did during the war and he replied, "We went behind enemy lines and made a nuisance of ourselves." That was all he ever said to me about his war-time exploits.

Joe got married after the war to Aunty Amy (whom I never met). She was a bit older than him. They had no children and sadly, she died after a few short years together.

For the remainder of his life, he cut a lonely figure, with just his dog to keep him company. He had family near by who looked after him when he became ill.

My last memory of him was pushing him around in a wheel chair which belonged to the hospice where he stayed until the end, 1988. It is such a pity he didn't get to read the tribute to him provided by his great friend, PcT Ted Robinson in this book.

Pct Terrence Douglas Gargan (1921 – 1998) SAS Operation Galia No.2 Stick:

Contribution from Terry Gargan's brother, John Gargan

Terry (known as Ted, Terry or 'the boy bandit' to the Rossenasi) joined the Army in 1936 aged just 15 years. Following basic training he was sent to India having been appointed as a Trumpeter. In 1940 he found himself in Egypt with the Ghurkhas. Terry spoke Hindustani having spent his early childhood in India.

Terry was seriously wounded by shrapnel at Tobruk in 1942 and taken prisoner. This was the first occasion he was captured but he managed to escape by stealing an ambulance and driving it back to the Allied lines in Egypt.

In hospital in Alexandria, doctors removed most of the shrapnel from his back but some remained lodged in position for the rest of his life. In 1943 Terry volunteered for the Army Air Corps and was sent to Achnacarry Commando Training Centre near Fort William. Part of this training involved being "dumped" in the south of England with a colleague but no money and told to return to Achnacarry within a limited time using their initiative.

Having past that test, Terry was next sent to Aldershot where, through boredom, he got into a spot of bother when he took and crashed an officer's car. On release from the "glass house" he was taken to Portsmouth where he found that he had been "volunteered" for a new unit called the Special Air Service. He did his parachute training at Manchester (Ringway) aerodrome.

Following one of his trips to France he returned to visit our sister, who lived
in Edinburgh, bringing with him, as a present, a yellow parachute. Parachute silk, he said, delighted the girls in France because they could make pretty underwear from them. Our sister Phyl was not keen on this idea.

In 1944, from an aircraft, Terry dropped propaganda leaflets of an obscene nature to the Germans as they were retreating. This was designed to demoralise the soldiers. Next, in Dec 1944 he dropped with the rest of the squad behind the lines into Rossano as part of Operation Galia.

In April 1945, Terry (along with Stanley Hann and other Galia members) took part in Operation Blimey where he was captured and (again) escaped, this time apparently bringing his Italian prison guard with him.

Terry saw active service in Palestine in 1946. In 1948 he was with the Rhine Army in Germany. Between stints with the SAS, Terry became a merchant seaman in 1950 for a short time. In 1954 he was again called up to fight in the jungles of Malaya. Next he was called up for the Suez emergency in 1956 but didn't get any further than Cyprus.

Throughout his service career, Terry oscillated up and down the NCO ranks. It seems the army found him to be both good and bad. He was finally released from Reserve Service in 1959.

Terry's family life after Army service could best be described as turbulent. Two wives and six children. In the 1960's, Terry thought he would visit his mother and our sisters in Australia, however he was refused a British passport on the grounds that he was born in, what is now, Pakistan. Our father was born in Ireland and served in the British Army in India when Terry was born. Terry was very annoyed at this decision but refused to pursue it further.

In civilian life, Terry worked as a night security guard for a cake factory in Manchester.

Contribution from
Ken and Rosemari
Penman – related to
partisans crucial to
the success of SAS
Operation Galia

Angelo Pietro
(Jock) Sartori

Born in Cupar, Scotland to Italian parents, Jock was educated at primary school in Cupar until the age of 11 when he was sent in early 1938 to complete his education in Italy at the Instituto Salesiano San Benedetto in Parma. He stayed at the School until early 1944 when he was advised to leave as the Germans were taking an interest in the school and its pupils at that time. He then joined his Grandfather in the village of Buzzo near Albareto.

Jock was recruited into the International Battalion by Major Gordon Lett on 1st August 1944 after having spent a short time as a Partisan with the Centro Croce brigade under the leadership of Richetto. Whilst with the Partisan group Jock met Lt Geoff Lockwood who, recognising his value as an interpreter, recommended him to Major Lett.

As he spoke fluent English and Italian, Jock soon proved his worth and became a valued member of Major Lett's group, being used as a courier, guide and interpreter by the Major until the end of the war.

We (his family) know from snippets of information gleaned from Jock that he took part in Operation Galia, and was used as a guide and an interpreter for a number of SAS actions. Jock recalled being fired at from very close range by a German machine gun at Buzzo and spoke of the 2 German prisoners taken at Sero. He also recalled hiding in a cave in the mountains with some of the SAS paratroopers when the German troops were searching for them.

After the men of Operation Galia exfiltrated from the Rossano area, Jock (at the age of 17) was placed in charge of the squad of men from Buzzo and remained at the Major's side in Rossano until eventually crossing the lines with Lt Lockwood, as part of an advance party, to SOE headquarters in Florence where they were joined shortly afterwards by Major Lett.

After a short spell in Florence Jock was sent back behind enemy lines to re-join the men of the International Battalion and make preparations to support the advancing allied army. He and some of his men soon linked up again with Major Lett in La Spezia, providing support after the Major liberated that city, staying there until the Allied Military Government arrived.

After hostilities ended Jock and many other men of the International Battalion undertook the extremely hazardous task of clearing minefields that the Germans had laid around the city of Pontremoli before retreating. This proved to be a very dangerous job, one close friend of Jock's was killed and many other men suffered serious injuries. There were no mine detectors available. The men had to first locate the mines before attempting to disable them.

Throughout the years after the war Jock stayed in touch with many of the men he had forged friendships with, including Major Lett, SAS Pct Gordon (Lofty) Rose, Chris Leng (SOE) and the many Italian Partisans and the people of the Rossano valley, all of whom he would visit and spend time with whenever he returned to Italy and his beloved mountains of Rossano

Angelo passed away on 5th January 1979 at the age of 51. He was survived by his wife Ida, four daughters and two grand-daughters. Ida passed away in 1990. There are now five grandchildren and three great grandchildren. His family continue to visit the Buzzo area of Italy regularly, where the family originated, with frequent visits to Jock's beloved Rossano.

Bruno Zanre

A cousin of Jock Sartori, Bruno joined the International Battalion around the same time as Jock and was used as a courier and guide. He spent a few years working in London after the war before returning to Buzzo, where he married and lived out his life, Bruno died in October 2009

Little else is known of Bruno's activities with the International Battalion as, like many others, he didn't speak much about those times. During Galia, Lt Gibbon and his stick number 4 operated around the Buzzo area most of the time. Bruno Zanre was one of those who took them over to Buzzo from the Rossano valley at the end of December.

In the book "Centocroci per la Resistenza" by Camillo Del Maestro,
there is an article by Bruno Zanre, which reads:

" I became aware of the existence of armed partisans at Lago Pave in February '44 [Fermo and fifteen men] They were part of a local squad whose members worked in the fields and took up arms with Comandante Angelo Schiavetta. There were twenty of us, from Buzzo and Gotra, organised in the spring of '44, and we remained in this position until the end of the July rastrellamento, when I joined the International Battalion as a courier for Gordon Lett. The most important action with this phantom squadron was the participation in the battle of Manubiola...I was with the partisan command at Zaloni on 13th September, when the Alpini, under the pretext of a white flag set a trap for us: I remained for a good 13 hours in the water of the Gotra river. When I was able to get out, during a lull in the shooting, I got to the road, and was able to mount a motorcycle and sidecar that carried arms and munitions, and was able to take it to Boschetto. In March 1945, I was part of the Allied Mission in the IV Operative Zone, making contact with various formations. It was dangerous work. Of 15 couriers, 10 were killed."

Louis
Pippo Siboldi

One of the outstanding characters from the partisans who took part in Operation Galia was Pippo Siboldi. Pippo's house in Sero became battle HQ during the Galia mission. Although middle aged at the time of Galia, Pippo was very fit, knew the terrain very well and having lived in America for a time, spoke passable English which was a great advantage to the Galia squad. Pippo proved himself so invaluable to the SAS during the mission that after helping to lead the Galia squad to safety at the end of the Operation, he volunteered to join the SAS and then parachuted back to Italy to take part in SAS Operation Tombola. Brian Lett's book 'SAS in Tuscany' gives more details about this remarkable Italian patriot and hero.

Major Rooney – OIC 3 Squadron, 2 SAS

Contribution from Chris Rooney – son of Major Rooney

Although Major Rooney did not parachute into Rossano with the men of Galia - as officer in charge of 3 Squadron 2 SAS he would have played a crucial role in the operation and support of the mission. He was copied into the operational orders replicated in appendix 1 of this book. His experience as a commando with numerous behind the lines adventures to his name was so valued that there is evidence the Galia operation was delayed to await his arrival in Italy prior to Christmas 1944.

My Father's full name was Oswald Basil Rooney called after his father Basil Oswald Rooney, born November 1916, in the middle of the first World War. Major Rooney was 'renamed' by a barmaid during the war as 'Mickey' after the diminutive American actor. He had lost an uncle at Gallipoli in May 1915 and also an uncle by marriage at Paschendale in 1917, neither of these deaths were ever mentioned in the family.

My father left school in about 1934/1935 and went into the family business of Brush making in Walthamstow. He was a tough, strong man. For recreation, he played Rugby in the winter and cricket in the summer. He joined the East India and Sportsman club which, at that time, was the centre of English Rugby. There he met Basil O'Brien who was a cousin of Rochford, a school friend. In 1939, he was playing for the Harlequins who had 8 of the English team in the side His ambition was to play Rugby for England and he may well have succeeded had the war not intervened.

In September 1939 Basil O'Brien and he joined the 21st Artist Rifles (their army numbers are consecutive). They both had a certain amount of Corp training at school Basil had attended Stonyhurst. Having done their training they were posted into the Scots Guards as Guardsmen.

Basil O'Brien knew how to Ski, so when an opportunity to go to Chamonix and ski at the Army's expense came up, they both volunteered. This is how they ended up in the 5th Battalion of the Scots Guards, with a number of other Characters who keep appearing later in the war: both Stirling brothers (David and Bill), Lord Lovat, Pinckney, Calvert, Scratchley, Jellicoe, Spencer-Chapman and others

The Ski battalion was disbanded after training and my father and Basil applied to join a Regiment that had been disbanded many years before. The army were not amused and sent them off to The Inniskillling in Omagh Northern Island. This is where he met my mother who was in the British army, even though she came from southern Ireland.

Major Rooney was an excellent leader of men. By late 1944 however, the war and years of living dangerously had taken its toll on his physical condition making active participation in the field impossible. Instead, Major Rooney brought his vast experience to bear by taking responsibility for training many of the men in 3 squadron 2 SAS including the men who were to become the Galia squadron. As one of the most experienced commandos in the SAS at the time of Operation Galia and as one of the senior officers in the SAS, Major Rooney would have played a key role in the planning, authorisation, organisation and maintenance of the essential logistical support to the troops in the field, not just for Galia but for many of the SAS Operations in Italy which took place in 1944/45.

After the war my father just wanted to lead a normal life. He lived in Essex, worked in London and brought up five children. When demobbed, he went back into the family brush making business. He then went to work for a number of other companies: Courage Breweries, Trans World Bowling, Charringtons on the Hotel side and then back to finish off in the Brush business again.

My father died in 1995. By this time his back, damaged when dropping into Metz was giving him a lot of trouble.

Having read the book on Blair 'Paddy' Mayne "Rogue Warrior of the SAS" I asked why he was so successful and had managed to stay alive despite the odds. He said Paddy Mayne had trained his men again and again, until he knew exactly what they would do under pressure, just like a Rugby team (Paddy of course was a rugby international before the war).

Sergeant Trevor Harrold

Trevor 'Trev' Harrold was one of the men in Ltn Shaunnessy's Number 5 stick on Galia who was captured by the Brigata Nera on new years eve/new year's day 1944/45.

Soon after the war ended, my father employed Trev in his brush making factory 'R.A. Rooney limited' in Walthamstow, North London. My father always said Trev was a very good organiser. Trevor worked at the brush factory for the rest of his working life, eventually taking over as factory manager. He lived in Walthamstow and was a great supporter of his local cricket club. Trev married and had a son, I think called John who went into banking and there was also a daughter but we haven't heard from Trev or his family for some years now.

Corporal John Matthews – SAS Operation Galia –

Contribution from Hank and Glenda Robinson (Glenda is John's daughter)

My Father, Corporal John Matthews was Born 29/04/1920 and Married Irene Lawson in June 1945 in Ilford Essex London England. John and Irene had three children: Rosalind born in England; Glenda in New Zealand in 1954 and John in New Zealand in 1957.

They now have 8 grand children and 7 great grand children. John became restless after the War and after a few years with jobs like the Telephone exchange in 1952 he decided emigrate to New Zealand and join the New Zealand army. With the promise of a great life, John went on ahead of Irene and his first born daughter Rosalind, who followed him out there a few months later. The initial position offered to him in the NZ Army turned out to be with the catering corps - a far cry (as we now know) from his former life with the SAS.

The family's living conditions on arrival were primitive to say the least and at times they had no electricity or running water. My father was not one to give up easily and he moved around different units in Auckland trying to provide better living conditions for his wife and growing family. During his NZ army tenure he was also engaged in training those called up for compulsory military service (since abolished). He was hugely respected by the men he trained and I have memories of young men greeting him on the street in Auckland years after the training exercises. After about 10 years of service with the NZ Army, dad became ill and he had to leave the Army abruptly. We became virtually homeless while he recuperated. My mother (Irene) took on a 'live in' housekeeping position where we stayed for a few months until 1962. Dad managed to get a job with the Electricity Dept – a Government Dept – when he recovered.

Simultaneously, they built a house and settled into family life. He became involved in football as John Jnr played for a local club. My father later went on to coach senior teams. He was always totally committed to everything he took on and as honest as can be. He is still a life member of this Football Club. He remained in this house until he retired from his position at the age of 65. A couple of years after retirement they sold up and moved to their current residence near the Sea. Both were keen walkers and they spent many years exploring the coast line.

In his mid eighties John began to develop the early signs of dementia and his condition has recently deteriorated.   I have been trying desperately to recall anything specific he said about his SAS days but unfortunately it is almost as if is life in England was a chapter in a book that closed when he got on that boat to New Zealand. He never talked about the SAS very much at all but always had the SAS shield on the wall. I recall him often mentioning the regimental motto "who dares wins". He also talked about the great rivalry he had with his brother Arthur who was a paratrooper during the war.

He would say to Arthur "Once you got across enemy lines you were just infantry but our regiment would run around causing havoc". He was hugely proud of this. He would talk more about his early Army days when his father, an ex-army man marched him in and had him enlisted as a trumpeter at a very young age. (He still has this trumpet). His father also gave the army his blessing to discipline his son as required and his very early days were quite brutal as he struggled to conform. He learned how to get by and talked about things like making his bed in the immaculate way they did and then sleeping on the floor so he could pass inspection in the morning. He would also put on that posh 'sergeant major' voice to relay how he was spoken to and which apparently led to his nick-name of 'Sir John' during his SAS years.

My father met my mother in the Army – she was on radar and he on guns. She accidently spilled a beer on him in the officer's mess during a break and to his delight unexpectedly promptly bought him a replacement. It was love at first sight and they married as soon as the war was over. Mum's parents wouldn't let her get married any earlier. It is hard to believe they are now both 92 and have been married 67 years. As children we were never privy to any personal information about them. They were and still are extremely private and independent.

Author's note

Sergeant Leonard ('Chalky') Wright MM, Number 1 stick Galia

Sergeant Chalky Wright was my father's stick commander on Galia. He also took part in other SAS Operations including some with Ted Robinson. The disbandment of the SAS so soon after the end of the war meant that many war-time members simply lost touch with friends and comrades with whom they had shared so much hardship and adventure.

At one of the SAS re-union lunches attended by my father and Lofty Kennedy in 1993, my Dad was told by one of his old friends that Chalky Wright had been trying to contact 'Spam' for several years in the 1980s but had been writing to an address we had moved away from years before. He also discovered that Chalky had been living in Sheffield at the same time I was living there, undergoing my training as a lawyer. Sadly his letters never reached Dad and they never got the opportunity to chew over old times. He found out at the 1993 re-union lunch that Chalky Wright had passed away in the mid-eighties.

I discovered, after the first edition of this book had been published, that Chalky Wright had been awarded the Military Medal for his part in Operation Galia. The citation for his Military Medal reads as follows:

"This NCO was a member of a troop dropped by parachute behind enemy lines on the 27th December 1944. During the Operations lasting between the 27th December 1944 to 20th February 1945 the conduct of this NCO was outstanding. He was present during every major attack and his calm steady manner in the face of enemy fire and prompt obedience to all orders given by his officers whatever the dangers involved in carrying them out, cannot be too highly praised. He particularly distinguished himself on the 11th January 1945 when taking part in an ambush on the Genoa-La Spezia Road near Bocca Del Pignone. Of the 30 Germans killed and wounded at least three were personally accounted for by him. With complete disregard for his own personal safety, in the face of accurate enemy fire, he calmly stayed in position directing the fire of an MMG. In Arctic conditions, his physical strength in carrying a member of the troop ill with pneumonia through deep snow drifts to safety, and his general conduct and leadership throughout the operation are worthy of the highest praise."

Signed

R Walker Brown, Major

The trooper ill with pneumonia is almost certainly PcT Eric (Lofty) Kennedy who was in Chalky's stick along with Spam, PcT Reg Everett and Corporal Johnson, the radio operator.

Eric and his wife Sally visited my parents in 1993, travelling from their adopted home in Canada to stay with my mother and father at their home in Frinton, Essex. My mother recalls how Eric (Lofty) greeted my father when they met at the airport after so many years:

"Always very theatrical with his words and actions and still speaking with a strong Austrian accent, Lofty embraced Stan   telling me over and over again 'Stanley, he saved my life! He carried me over the mountains when I was sick with pneumonia. He wouldn't leave me to be shot by the Nazis."

Dad, in typical fashion, was a bit embarrassed by Lofty's emotional greeting and played down what he had said. My Mother also couldn't imagine how Stan, at 5 foot 9 inches could have possibly carried Lofty at 6 foot 4 inches up and down the ice clad mountains with full kit whilst being pursued by hostile forces. The likelihood, given Chalky's citation above, is that Lofty Kennedy's kit, weapon and ammunition would have been shared out between Spam, Reg Everett and Chalky (Johnson may or may not have been present). The men probably took turns to support or carry their mate, rather than leave him behind to take his chances in a cave or sheltering with villagers at the height of the enemy search and destroy action. It also seems likely that at some stage Chalky, who was much stockier and taller than my Dad, may also have had to physically carry Lofty draped over his shoulders when he became unconscious or was too sick to support himself.

Stanley and Lily Hann meeting Lofty Kennedy in 1993 for the 50th anniversary celebrations of the formation of the SAS. After the war Kennedy moved to Canada following the discovery that his family in Austria had become victims of Hitler's Final Solution.

Acknowledgements

Over the course of the past five years, I have met many people both in Italy and in the UK who have assisted me on my journey of discovery about SAS Operation Galia. I have made great friends along the way, such as Omar Buchioni, nephew of General Dani Buchioni, one of the veteran partisan commanders who assisted Galia.

I simply could not have written this book without the goodwill, help and assistance of Brian Lett QC (son of Major Gordon Lett, DSO). Brian's comprehensive knowledge of Italy, its turbulent history during WW2, his Father's activities behind the lines with the partisans and Operation Galia, must, today, be unrivalled. Through his annual treks across the rugged, mountainous, spectacular terrain of the Northern Apennines, Brian opened my eyes to the incredible feats of endurance and survival undertaken by the men of SAS Operation Galia. He introduced me to veteran partisans and characters like Lino Moggia ('I knew your father'), Giovani Tongnatelli (the Miller), the Deluchi family (whose parents greeted the men of Galia with - of all things - a cup of tea on landing) and Dimmo Baldissini (the Italian liaison officer who parachuted, with my Father, back into Rossano on Operation Blimey). Through Brian, I came to understand and appreciate the incredible bravery, suffering and sacrifice that the local Italian people had to endure before, during and after Operation Galia. Since the first publication of this book Brian Lett has published his own valuable contribution to the history of the SAS, namely 'SAS in Tuscany' (Pen and Sword). From a historic perspective, Brian's book examines and compares several wartime SAS Italian operations. I would have no hesitation in recommending Brian's book as companion reading to SAS Operation Galia.

I would also pay tribute to Gordon Lett's memoire of his time behind the lines as an escaped PoW acting for SoE - 'Rossano (An adventure of the Italian Resistance)'. This book contains several Chapters devoted to the Galia Operation including the original parachute drop and subsequent guerrilla campaign. Written by one of the chief protagonists, I could not hope to improve upon such a valuable, historic account of these events. 'Rossano' has been a source of inspiration for SAS Operation Galia. Indeed, the basic premise of my book, was to tell, for the first time, the whole story of SAS Operation Galia from the surviving records and first hand accounts.

The other main source material was Captain Bob Walker Brown's excellent debrief report of Galia written soon after the Operation. The following sentence in that report revealed the fact that my Father appeared to be one of only two parachutists who linked both main SAS groups (one led by Walker Brown, the other by Major Lett) during the height of the enemy search and destroy action during January 1945:

"Pcts. Everett and Hann who had been sent out to make a recce of our line of march did not succeed in rejoining the main body for some days"

From Rossano and other sources, it is now clear that my father and his great friend Reg Everett somehow succeeded in dodging the enemy patrols which were combing the mountains for them and their comrades, to link up with Major Lett and his group at Sero. Thus, if my Father had been alive today, he would have been in a position to tell the story of Galia from this unique perspective. Of course, it is now hugely frustrating for me, to realise that I spent the best part of forty years with access to no less than two original Galia squad members (my Dad and Jimmy Church) but for whatever reason, I didn't discover their respective stories until both had passed away. I am very fortunate that, thanks mainly to both Gordon and Brian Lett, some tangible record of Galia remained for me to stumble across, however belatedly.

The Monte San Martino Trust is a fine charitable institution founded by another great man I have had the privilege to meet, namely J. Keith Killby OBE.

Keith is an SAS 'original' who saw action and was captured on more than one occasion in Italy during the War. However, although he faced great danger along with all other SAS troops, due to his beliefs and attached to the medical corps, Keith obtained special dispensation from his commanding officer never to carry arms. Keith founded the Monte San Martino Trust in 1989 largely to say 'thank you' to the Italian people who had, at great risk to themselves, helped not only Keith, but thousands of other Allied escapees during 1943-5. Amongst other things, the Trust organise 'freedom trail' treks across war-time escape routes to raise sponsorship and funding. I have included details of the Trust in this book in the hope that readers will consider participating with the Trust in some way.

I am also indebted to free-lance reporter and military historian, Jon Cooksey who accompanied me on my first trip to Rossano and who so eloquently penned an article with me which subsequently appeared in 'Britain at War' Magazine in July 2008. Jon is a historian, writer and editor of many military books and publications. His encouragement and editorial skills have been a very valuable source of assistance to me.

Similarly, I am grateful to David Belbin, Graham Joyce (lecturers on my Creative Writing MA course, Nottingham Trent University 2007/08) and to my fellow students, many of whom helped to critique early draft chapters of this book.

It has been wonderful to meet Ted Robinson and his family and to hear first hand from a Galia veteran at last, stories about my Dad and Galia, including my Father's war-time nickname 'Spam'. In the process, we may have also discovered a Galia participant who was not named in the official roll of SAS men who took part.

Ted has a copy of the classic Galia photo provided (we believe) to all Galia parachutists. On the back are the signatures of several Galia veterans, including 'Spam'. Another of the signatures is of Don Hempstead, one of my Dad's SAS pals who appears in several of Dad's other war-time photographs, but is not named in Walker Brown's debrief report. My mother tentatively identified Don Hempstead as one of the parachutists in the classic Galia line-up (the photograph on the cover of this book). She also confirmed Don passed away many years ago. A month before this book was due to be completed an SAS association member got in touch and forwarded the definitive personnel list of parachutists who took part in Galia. Among that list is the name 'Don Hemptead'. I am pleased to be able to put to rest that minor mystery and provide Don with some much over-due recognition for his part in Galia.

Whilst I have tried to write the full story of Galia, alas, I realise, (having only met Ted Robinson in 2009 (just prior to publication of the first edition of this book), that his experiences were different again from those of my Father. Ted Robinson was one of the youngest SAS paratroopers in the Galia squad but had already seen plenty of action having parachuted into France on D-Day, along with my father's stick Sergeant, Chalky Wright. Ted was one of the wireless operators the SAS HQ stick who were relentlessly pursued by the enemy for "59 continuous hours without rest or rations" covering huge distances across mountainous terrain, until they holed up, just North of the village of Buzzo to wait for the rastrellamento to run its course.

It has been a great pleasure to meet Ted and his wife and their adult children, Alan, Sheila and Julia (the latter apparently being named after Ted's Galia wireless code call sign 'Julia is a little girl'). It is my sad duty to report in this second edition, that Ted Robinson passed away in January 2012 following a short illness but surrounded by his loving family. The Robinsons, along with other relatives of Galia parachutists have kindly submitted additional information about Galia which is contained in a new chapter 'Roll Call'. Ted Robinson also penned a personal message in th first edition which I have replicated in the Roll Call chapter. I am very grateful to all those members of the extended Galia family who have submitted contributions to this section.

It was a bitter blow in the final stages of writing the first edition, to learn that Bob Walker Brown had passed away in August 2009. It is obvious from everything I have heard and read that my Father's commanding officer was an incredible leader and a very brave man. What comes across to me is the sense that, although he had a job to do, he really cared about his men and would never have taken unnecessary risks with their lives. The fact that all the Galia squad returned alive is a testament to his extra-ordinary leadership, determination and courage. Unfortunately, he did not enjoy good health in the final years of his life and so I was never able to meet him in person. I was at least able to speak to him by mobile phone when in Sero on my first visit:

"Your dad was a fine soldier. I remember him well."

I have included, in the new Roll Call Chapter, the obituary which appeared in the Daily Telegraph on Friday, September 18th 2009 which contains a comprehensive summary of SAS Operation Galia, Bob Walker Brown's military career and his many other achievements. Unfortunately, the obituary contained a couple of inaccurate statements about Galia which Brian Lett was quick to correct in a follow up letter. This letter too is included to keep the record straight.

I consider myself very fortunate to have reached the market with this book having won a competition. Long may the Impress Awards continue to give encouragement to enthusiastic, novice scribblers like myself. Whilst the publishing rights are now back with the author (via Hann Books Limtied). I remain grateful to Impress for their help and support with the first edition.

The published works I have used to research the facts are listed. Italy's Sorrow by James Holland, The SAS by Philip Warner and Sterling's Men by Gavin Mortimer are worthy of special mention along with Major Roy Farran's war-time memoir 'Winged Dagger'. As mentioned, Brian Lett has published SAS in Tuscany since the first edition and some minor revisions have been necessary following further research and discoveries made by Brian.

2005 -2007 was a difficult time for me from a health perspective and I wish to express my deep gratitude to my GP (Dr Nick Hutchinson) and the specialists and staff at the City Hospital, Nottingham (particularly Mr A.P. Broodryk, Orthopaedic Surgeon and Dr Philip Courtney, Consultant Rheumatologist) for rebuilding me and getting me back on my feet. Thanks to them, I have been able to visit Italy on several occasions to undertake research and, at last, to fully participate in the 2009 Monte San Martino Freedom trail traversing the mountain paths and goat tracks from Pontremoli via Rossano and Sero to Levanto, a distance of some forty-five or so miles.

I must here make mention of members of my family who have helped me discover valuable clues to Galia. My mother Lilian, in particular, for providing me with all of Dad's photos some of which (according to Ted Robinson) were taken by Dad during Operation Galia. I don't believe these photographs have ever appeared before and I hope they will become a valuable addition to the SAS archive. My elder brothers, Michael and David, Winnie Church and my Mother have all helped to fill in much needed family history and anecdotes some of which are recorded in these chapters.

My wife Sarah has been a constant support, not least, by allowing me to undertake two unaccompanied trips to Italy to research this book and to enjoy walking in the mountains etc while she stayed at home to look after our boys and continued working.

As for my lads, William and Joseph, this book has been written with them very much in mind - to give them an insight into the character of the granddad they never got to know. To show how history and the 'might have beens' can still influence or affect our lives today and lastly, to always remember the debt our generation and subsequent generations owe to my Father and all those like him who 'did their bit'.

To all those friends, family, work mates and acquaintances too numerous to name individually who have in some way assisted me with this book, I would like here to express my sincere gratitude.

Finally, This book is written first and foremost as a tribute to my father and all the men of Operation Galia. Although I have tried my best to avoid mistakes or inaccuracies in the historical record, I am not (and do not purport to be) a historian. I have, however, striven to record the story accurately from the information available to me. If mistakes have been made or are subsequently discovered, I confess - they are mine and mine alone.

Rob Hann   2013

Appendix 1
Operation order No. 1: Operation Galia

Copy No: ....

OPERATION 'GALIA'

Operation Order No. 1.

Information about the enemy.

A. Enemy troops on the West coast of Italy are very thin on the ground, and are located as follows:-

1. From the Appenines to the sea – 281 Regiment, consisting of 2 German battalions.

2. From the Appenines to the North of Pistoia, map reference 14, is the Monti Rosa Italian Division, consisting of 2 Italian fascist alpine regiments. This formation also has elements between Spezia and Repallo on the coast.

3. 16th S.S. recce battalion is operating along the main road including armoured half tracks. One squadron has 6 infantry guns and about the same number of heavy mortars.

4. Spezia is garrisoned by the 135 Fortress brigade, consisting of 903, 904, 905, 906, and 907 Fortress battalions each approximately 500 strong. This brigade supplies reinforcements to units at the front.

5. Aulla. Aulla is a focal point of 3 main roads and is garrisoned by rear echelons of 281 regiment, estimated strength 300 men.

B. Recently there has been an extensive drive by the Germans against the large groups of Italian partisans in the North Appenines. This has left the partisans in a very much weakened state in many cases, since they have now been in the field in open guerrilla warfare for nearly a year, and morale is considerably reduced owing to the failure of the last Allied attack. Food in the mountains is short.

The formations the Germans have used for this drive are as follows:-

162 Turkoman division.
1 battalion of parachute reinforcements, which has operated along the line of the Piacenza-Genoa road.
Several Italian fascist formations.

Information about own troops.

A. Partisans

Partisans in this area consist of the 1st Ligurian-division, and are centred around Monte Pichiana. This division has not to date been attacked by the Germans, but is the only partisan formation in this area which has not been. It is therefore expected that it will be attacked soon.

It is commanded by a very able Italian Commander called 'Turchi' (Col Fontana). He is advised by a major, Gordon Lett, an escaped P.W. previously in the Indian Army and now official B.L.O. to this formation. His code name is Blundel Violet, and he is in wireless contact with Monopoli.

The 1st Ligurian division has received about 30 tons of stores since the beginning of the month; the last drop made on the 16th. There is very little food in this area and living conditions are hard.

The partisans have blown several road bridges around the area, which is about 7 miles square, to cut off as much as possible from German attack.

To the North and almost joining the 1st Ligurian division area is a rather larger partisan group called the Commando Unico, which is centred around the area Monte Bello. They were previously at Bottola, but were driven out by the Germans on the 5th December, and it is thought they have now dispersed into many small bands.

B. Own Forces with Partisans

There is –

(1) An O.S.S. Italian team called Liberta, and B.L.O. Gordon Lett in the 1st Ligurian division area.

(2) There is an American O.G. called Walla Walla 2978 towards Warzi.

(3) There is an American O.G. code name Nembo, North of Rapallo near Genoa.

(4) There is an American O.G. called Tina 9851.

(5) There is a B.L.O. code name Cayusa, consisting of Lieut Formicelli plus 6 men at 7160.

C. <u>Own troops in front line</u>

Facing the Germans on the West coast is the 1st American Negro division.

<u>Other Intelligence.</u>

a.   Enemy transport usually moves only by night.

b.   The railway between Parma and Spezia, which is the only one in this area, is not believed to be used.

c.   Partisans in the Ligurian area have received stores by mule trains infiltrating through the lines into their area. The journey <u>takes approximately a week.</u>

<u>General Object</u>

A detachment of approximately 30 all ranks No. 2 SAS Regiment will be dropped in the area North of Spezia, to operate with partisans (1st Ligurian division), and harass the enemy lines of communication in this area.

The timing will be tied up with the projected 5th Army attack, with the object of:-

(a) Influencing the enemy to hold troops in the area, and result in reinforcements not being sent to the main battle area Modena-Bologna.

(b) Delaying any enemy withdrawals along the routes Spezia – Parma and Reggio – Emilia.

The S.A.S. party, if not over-run by the 5th Army, will infiltrate back through the enemy lines in due course.

<u>Intention</u>

To drop 3 sticks of 10 parachutists to reception, on a D.Z. in the 1st Ligurian division area on the 22nd December, or the first fine day after that. These sticks will then split into 6 parties of 5, to operate against enemy road communications, either in conjunction with, or without partisans.

<u>Method</u>

If the situation as regards reception by partisans remains as at present, the party will be flown from Malignano, and dropped on:-

D.Z. Aydon – 14 miles North of Spezia, sheet 95 (P) 632335. Ground recognition – white parachutes in shape of T (or if snow, red parachutes) at 12.000 hrs on 22nd December, or first fine day after.

If there is no reception at Aydon, aircraft will drop if there is reception at Lifton near Boschetto 84/5762.

In the event of no wireless contact being made with either Blundel Violet or Liberta, party will be dropped in any case on Aydon or Lifton at 1600 hrs 22nd December.

The party will be ferried up from Brindisi to Malignano, where they will stage for the night, on the morning of 21st December.

Containers, etc.

Party will drop with rucksacks in leg bags, not weighing more than 60 lbs. Any extra kit which is required will be dropped in containers or packages. These containers will be packed at Brindisi, under the supervision of Sjt. Pearson, and flown up in the same aircraft which ferry the party up to Malignano.

It is suggested that at least three containers per aircraft should carry food (i.e. S.O.M. pre-packed containers) since food is very short in this area.

It should be stated now what articles will be required on re-supply, so that the containers may be pre-packed at once, and flown up to Malignano. Re-supply can only be done on an average once a week at this time of the year, so it is essential to seize the first good weather day. It will not be possible therefore, except in exceptional cases for special articles to be dropped quickly after they have been asked for.

There will also be delay in ferrying up containers after packing from Brindisi, until arrangements can be made to establish our own packing station at Malignano.

Evacuation

Party will exfiltrate back through the lines (if not over-run by 5th Army).

1. On orders from 15th Army Group or 5th Army, or

2. If enemy activity is such that forces can no longer operate successfully in the area.

Main objectives

1. Road Aulla – Parma.

2. Road Aulla – Reggio Nell Emilia.

3. A coast road Genoa – Spezia – Sarzana.

4. Main Parma road.

Note – Aulla is a focal point.

Inter-Communications

(a) Two Nicholls sets will be dropped with the party. There will be only one station worked by two W/T operators.

(b) Each party of 5 will carry one midget receiver to enable them to listen to orders and information broadcast from London.

There will obviously be a delay in passing this information back to London by signal from control set at Monopoli.

(c) There will be two control sets; one at the S.O.M. base at Monopoli, and one at the advanced No. 1 Special Force base at Florence. Both these stations will listen on the same frequency, and have the same one time pad. The station at Florence will take control as soon as satisfactory inter-communication is established.

(d) Intelligence from the field will be passed on immediately from control station to 5th Army, 15th Army Group and M.A.T.A.F.

Note – See Major Astor's detailed W/T orders re frequencies, crystals, codes and times.

Administration

1. All operational parties will have kit packed and weighed by the night of the 20th December. Containers and packages must also be ready by this time. Parachutes will have to be drawn from Station 54, Brindisi.

2. Major Farran or Major Rooney will arrange road transport from Monopoli to Brindisi on the 21st December.

3. A lecture on security will be given by Capt Walker-Brown, O.C. operational party, before the party is briefed.

4. The party will be briefed on the 21st December.

5. Operational money totalling 1,500 pounds, in lire, will be drawn by Capt Walker-Brown from No. 1 Special Force, and distributed amongst the party as he thinks fit.

6. On return from operation, party will report to No. 1 Special Force Advance Base, Florence.

19 Dec 44	Major, O.C. Det 2 SAS Regt.

Distribution:-	Copy No. 1 & 2	– G(Ops) B, 15 Army Gp
	3	– Adv HQ (G Ops) 5th Army
	4	– S.O.M. Mola
	5	– No. 1 Special Force
	6	– Major Rooney, O.C. 3 Sqn 2 SAS
	7 & 8	–Lt-Col Profumo.

APPENDIX 2
Report on Operation Galia

by Captain Walker Brown

OPERATION – 'GALIA'

Unit: 2 SAS Regt

1. Role: To harass the enemy in the area inland from SPEZIA.
2. Comd: Major R. WALKER BROWN DSO MBE.
3. Associated Jed teams: -
4. Date of first drop: 27 Dec 44
5. Date operation terminated: 15 Feb 45
6. Initial DZ: 647354
7. Reports submitted by: Major WALKER BROWN
8. Serial numbers of bombing targets submitted: -
9. Serial numbers of bombing targets known to have been attacked: -

10. Operational strength:	Number dropped	Number Infiltrated	Total
Officers	5	-	5
Ors:	28	-	28
	33	-	33

11. Casualties	Killed	Missing or PW	Wounded
Officers:		later	
Ors:			

12. Supplies dropped:
    (a) Containers:
    (b) Panniers   later
    (c) Packages
    (d) Jeeps
    (e) Other stores or eqpt

OPERATIONAL GALIA

NOMINAL ROLL OF PERSONNEL

TROOP HQ

Captain	R. Walker Brown, M.B.E.
Captain	Milne, R.A.M.C.
Cpl.	Lidington.
Cpl.	Cunningham.
Pct.	Robinson.
Pct.	Mathews.
Pct.	Mulvey.
Pct.	Rose.

No. 1 Stick.
Sgt. Wright.
Cpl. Johnson.
Pct. Kennedy.
Pct. Hann.
Pct. Everett.

No. 2 Stick
Lieut. Riccomini.
Pct. Gargan.
Pct. Shanley.
Pct. Sumptor.
Pct. Hildage.

No. 3 Stick.
Sgt. Rookes.
Pct. Duggan.
Pct. Taylor.
Pct. Tate.

No. 4 Stick
Lieut. Gibbon.
Cpl Ford.
Cpl. Larley.
Pct. Donnie.
Pct. Whittaker.

No.5 Stick.
Lieut. Shaughnessy.
Sgt. Harrold.
Cpl. Benson.
Pct. Phillips.
Pct. Church.
Pct. Mitchell.

[Although not included in Walker Brown's list of those who took part in Galia, it is now certain that Pct. Don Hempstead dropped with the Galia squad and Sgt. Guscott joined the squad during the operation after treking over the mountains.]

OPERATION GALIA

This operation in the area inland from Spezia has been spectacular both in the results achieved against the enemy and the manner in which the difficulties of terrain and winter weather were surmounted.

It lasted for a period of nine weeks during which, from reports at present available, it is known that the following casualties were inflicted on the enemy:-

> 22 trucks and 2 trailers destroyed, one truck damaged: a minimum of between 100 and 150 total casualties inflicted on the enemy during various actions which included attacks on German marching columns and on the town of Borgeto.

The skilful use of 3″ mortar and Bren guns enabled large bodies of enemy to be engaged, and 59 hours marching without rest or rations over hills deep in snow gave the party sufficient mobility to shake off the German troops deployed for pursuit. Mules were invaluable for transport purposes.

S.A.S. casualties, according to information at present available, amount to 6 missing – now reported as P.W. – out of the total of 33 employed on the operation.

A full report will be issued when the whole party has been debriefed.

PRELIMINARY REPORT

on

OPERATION GALIA

By Capt. R. WALKER BROWN, M.B.E.

(Ref Maps: Italy 1: 100,000 – sheets 84 and 95.)
(All map references are North Italy Brown Grid P)

27 Dec 44 No. 1 Troop 3 Squadron disemplaned at 647354, near Rossano, on DZ "Huntsville". The DZ was unsuitable for dropping personnel and the following light casualties were sustained on the trip: – Pct. Hildage, Mulvey, and Shanely. Major Gordon Lett whom Captain Walker Brown knew as a POW in Camp O PG 21, was in charge of the reception on the ground. Approximately 25% of the S.A.S. equipment, food, etc. was stolen by partisans.

28 Dec 44 Lieut. Gibbon and his stick moved to the area of the Pontremoli – Aulla road, Lieut. Shaughnessy and stick to the area Aulla – Reggio, and Sgt. Rookes' party to the Pontremoli – Cisa road. Captain Walker Brown and the rest of the troop remained at Rossano to hide the stores and to establish liaison with Major Lett and the partisans. It was not possible to establish W/T communication because of the difficulty caused by the mountains.

29 Dec 44 Captain Walker Brown with Troup HQ, Lieut. Riccomini's and Sgt. Wright's sticks, proceeded to Pieve, 608299, with the 3" mortar and 35 HE bombs. There was still no W/T communication. Contact was established with the partisan Justice and Liberty Brigade.

30 Dec 44 Captain Walker Brown's party ambushed the road from Spezia to Genoa at 580235. 3 German vehicles were destroyed and 1 set on fire. An enemy armoured vehicle replied with heavy 20 mm MG fire. 3 enemy were killed instantly and one died later in Borgeto hospital. The number of wounded is unknown.

31 Dec 44 Captain Walker Brown's party withdrew to Sero, 600281.

1 Jan 45 Captain Walker Brown's party attacked the German and Fascist units in Borgeto di Varo, 584240, with the 3" mortar at a range of 1,100 yards. 34 HE bombs were fired and direct hits were obtained on a number of houses occupied by enemy troops. 2 German lorries drove down the road towards Borgeto and stopped on hearing mortar fire. Bren gunners moved forward a few hundred yards and destroyed both vehicles. During this attack a party of partisans, fourteen strong, from the Justice and Liberty Brigade, was placed under the command of the S.A.S. This party took up fire positions to the South of Borgeto with the intention of stopping the enemy withdrawing through the

mountains, in which they did not succeed. The number of casualties is not known. The entire enemy garrison withdrew from Borgeto and did not return for 24 hours. One car was destroyed by mortar bomb. The objects of the attack were as follows: – (a) To make the presence of the SAS known to the enemy in the quickest possible time. (b) To create uneasiness among the garrison troops on the Genoa – Spezia road and to cause them to be reinforced. (c) To stop enemy movement on the Spezia –Genoa road.

2 Jan 45 Captain Walker Brown's party returned to Rossano for resupply. Still no W/T intercommunication had been established. Lieut. Gibbon returned to Rossano for fresh orders, having observed that there was no movement of enemy on the Aulla – Pontremoli road. He was then sent back to join Sgt. Rookes.

3 Jan 45 Lieut. Riccomini proceeded towards the area Valeriano, 686152. W/T intercommunication was established and a request passed over for resupply. Lieut. Shaughnessy and the whole of his stick were reported captured in Montebello, 709201, by a party of Brigata Nera who were said to have been dressed in civilian clothes. The Italian guide was interrogated, tortured, and then shot by Brigata Nera while attempting to escape. Troop HQ was awaiting resupply but weather conditions were extremely bad. A signal was received from base that aircraft would not fly to "Huntsville". Reply was sent back that "Huntsville" was the only DZ possible in our area for the following reasons:–

(a) Easiest DZ for getting resupply to detached sticks as it was approximately in the centre of the troop operations area.

(b) Any enemy attacks against the SAS would have to have come through under partisan observation of whose warning system we made use.

4 Jan 45 Lieut. Riccomini mined the road on the bridge over the river at 690146 near Valeriano. A mine detonated during the night 4/5th Jan, destroying a German truck, killing 12 and wounding 8 according to subsequent information obtained. Sgt. Wright moved to Sero with the intention of ambushing the Spezia – Genoa road. Troop HQ was still awaiting resupply.

Weather conditions were very severe. It was cold and there was heavy snow on the ground. Icing conditions and snow on the mountain tracks made movement extremely difficult and tedious.

5th Jan 45 A signal was received to the effect that the Air Force would not fly to "Huntsville", but that supplies for the SAS would be dropped to DZ "Halifax".

6 Jan 45 Sgt. Wright's stick attacked an enemy staff car, killing a high Fascist official and wounding three other officers. This car was

reported by the partisans to be carrying 125 million lire. Lieut. Riccomini returned to Rossano with his stick.

7 Jan 45 Troop HQ was still awaiting resupply. An attempt was made to cancel the drop at "Halifax" but signals from base confirmed again that aircraft would not drop at "Huntsville" but would fly to "Halifax." Signals were again sent by Major Lett and Captain Walker Brown, pointing out that it would be impossible to move stores dropped to "Halifax" across the mountains to Troop HQ and to the detached sticks, owing to the fact that by now there was very heavy snow on the ground and it was totally impossible to get mules across the mountains.

8 Jan 45 No W/T intercommunication was established.

9 Jan 45 Signals were put out on "Huntsville" in the remote hope that aircraft might drop. Lieut. Riccomini moved to "Halifax" with his stick, collected Sgt. Wright's stick, and arranged the reception at "Halifax". An aircraft dropped resupply at "Halifax" at about 15.30 hrs. Captain Walker Brown and Troop HQ immediately moved to "Halifax", arriving there after five hours march. About 40% of this drop was stolen by the Communist Justice and Liberty Brigade from Pieve. This was largely owing to the fact that the drop was scattered over four square miles of country and it was impossible to control pilfering with the number of men available.

10 Jan 45 The day was spent trying to recover the stolen equipment from partisans. At 19.00 hrs Captain Walker Brown's party moved to Sero with the intention of carrying out a night ambush on the Genoa – Spezia road. This, however, was found to be impossible because of sheets of solid ice on the mountain tracks leading down to the valley through which the main road runs. The men were continually falling and making a considerable amount of noise. The night was spent at Sero.

11 Jan 45 Captain Walker Brown took a recce party consisting of Pcts. Rose, Shanley, and Sumptor, and carried out a recce of the road bridge over the river at L'Ago, 549251. The recce showed that this was a possible target and the amount of explosive required was estimated to be 300 lbs P.H.E. Sgt. Wright, Pcts. Hildage and Hann, returned to DZ "Halifax" to prepare the reception. Lieut. Riccomini and the remainder of the party moved to an ambush position at 565243. On returning from this recce the party took up a firing position 300 yards from the German Fascist HQ building in Borgeto di Varo and were about to open fire on 2 Fascists playing tennis in the road when a column of vehicles was heard moving down the road towards the main ambush party and through the town. It was decided not to open fire as the recce party had only one Bren, and to allow the column to reach the main ambush party which had five Brens. The vehicles, which were later fired on by the main ambush party, halted in Borgeto for

five minutes and were under close observation by the recce party. The column consisted of a captured British staff car with trailer, with 6 Germans including an officer, a 10-ten lorry with large trailer, loaded with white canvas packages, 2 ft cube, and 27 German troops and 5 women. A third vehicle turned into a side street in Borgeto and halted. The two leading vehicles left Borgeto and were engaged by the main ambush party. 32 Bren magazines were fired, both vehicles and trailers were totally destroyed, the 10-tonner and trailer being set on fire with incendiary rounds. 26 were killed.

12 Jan 45 A report was received from civilians that Blackshirts were burning houses in Brugnato, 585255, as a reprisal for the ambush of the 11th. Brugnato was a town at which the SAS party had halted on the way to the ambush. Captain Walker Brown's party moved off with 3″ mortar and Brens, and occupied a mortar position on the mountain within range of Brugnato, the road-over-river bridge between Brugnato and Borgeto, and the town of Borgeto. By attacking Borgeto twice it was anticipated that the enemy would be forced to take action in order to prevent a third attack, either by reinforcing his garrisons on the coast road or by attacking the SAS area with a large body of troops in order to clean up the area. In addition it was intended to prolong the attack as long as possible and prevent transport moving between Spezia and Genoa.

Immediately before the first bomb was fired a single Thunderbolt dive-bombed Borgeto and dropped a dud bomb. The SAS party fired three IDS bombs on the road leading out of the town of Brugnato. The enemy in Brugnato immediately began withdrawing towards the bridge and the river. They were engaged with mortar fire. An enemy party of platoon strength took up firing positions on the southern side of the bridge and opened fire with MG 42s. This platoon was mortared and withdrew into the hills in disorder. Small enemy parties attempting to ford the river were also engaged. A number of the enemy were reported drowned in the river, presumably after having been wounded by mortar splinters as the river is only 2 ft deep.

An enemy 20 mm MG position sited in the cemetery in Borgeto was then engaged with three rounds rapid from the mortar, one bomb landing directly on the MG which was put out of action and the crew killed. The enemy continued to fire heavily but ineffectively. The mortar was sited for indirect fire behind a crest. Groups of ten rounds rapid were fired at intervals against the town and the enemy positions in the hills around the town. The SAS Bren gunners with one Italian Breda MG moved forward and to a flank and fired 57 Bren magazines of tracer and ball at the town, one house being set on fire.

At 16.00 hrs all ammunition was expended except the reserve and the troop prepared to move. At the same time, four Thunderbolts arrived on the scene. Two dive-bombed the bridge between Borgeto and Brugnato and two straffed the road. This produced a very considerable effect on the Italians and also, presumably, the enemy who thought that the SAS party had fighter support at its disposal. The enemy then brought up a 105 mm field gun from Spezia and shelled the hillside very heavily. The gunners apparently did not know where the mortar position had been and no gunfire actually engaged the SAS mortar position.

No partisans took part in this attack with the exception of a number of brave men who discharged sten guns towards Borgeto at a range of 3,000 yards.

The SAS party withdrew in extended order up the mountain without casualties.

<u>13 Jan 45</u> Returned to DZ "Halifax" to find that a single B25 had dropped a Vickers MMG without a parachute.

<u>14 Jan 45</u> Waited all day for resupply but there was no drop owing to bad weather.

<u>15 Jan 45</u> Received a drop with two Vickers MGs. Moved to Rossano. Cpl. Johnson and two men with the remainder of the drop were left as the equipment and stores could not be carried that day owing to shortage of mules.

<u>16/17 Jan 45</u> The party rested and information was collected about the area of the Pontremoli – Aulla road.

<u>18 Jan 45</u> Captain Walker Brown's party, leaving behind the following sick: Pcts. Rose, Gargan and Hildage, moved to Codolo, 685400, with Major Lett, intending to carry out a Vickers gun attack against the German garrison of 300 in Vignola, 700416. This attack, however, had to be abandoned owing to the fact that the enemy had the route between Codolo and Vignola under observation. It was then decided to carry out an ambush on the road South of Pontremoli and immediately afterwards to attack the road North of Pontremoli. Accordingly, the SAS party moved to Arzelato, 691366, with the intention of leaving the mules at Arzelato and attacking the road that night. The march from Codolo to Arzelato was exceptionally hard and slow because there was heavy cloud, ice and snow, and it was pitch black. It was found that it would not be possible to attack the road that night and for the party to withdraw to a secure base by daylight. Therefore the following day was spent at Arzelato.

<u>19 Jan 45</u> All personnel had to remain in houses with no movement outside as Arzelato was under full observation of the enemy garrison of Pontremoli. On the night of the 19th, a party of partisans from the band of Ricchetta, who had asked permission from Major Lett to take part in an SAS attack, arrived and placed themselves under SAS command. The party of 20 was commanded by a partisan known as Nino, a man with a high reputation among the partisans.

At 19.00 hrs, in darkness, Captain Walker Brown's party and the partisans, less Major Lett, Cpl. Johnson, and the mules, attacked the Pontremoli – Aulla road at 744363. Owing to the bad light only two Vickers guns were used and both of these were sited to fire on fixed lines at a point where the road has a drop of 50 ft on the West flank and a steep cutting on the East flank. A single vehicle with headlights was engaged and drove straight into a column of marching troops who were also hit by MG fire. Casualties are not known but German troops told civilians the following day that there were large numbers of dead on the road. The enemy replied with very weak and totally ineffective rifle fire but it was sufficient to make the partisans disappear rapidly.

<u>20 Jan 45</u> At 00.30 hrs the SAS party and partisans withdrew from the ambush position and marched to Codolo. The partisans remained at Codolo and the SAS party moved to Noce, 632377, to an RV with Cpl. Johnson and the mules, arriving there at 06.00 hrs. An Italian runner sent from Major Lett met the party at the RV. He carried a message informing Captain Walker Brown that Cpl. Johnson and the mule train had made contact with an enemy patrol but had succeeded in withdrawing without incident to Arzelato where Major Lett had redirected them to Coloretta, 623370.

The SAS party accordingly marched to Coloretta, arriving at 07.00 hrs. The party was extremely tired. At 07.15 hrs, first light, a large force of Germans estimated at battalion strength were observed at 250 yards advancing in extended order. The alarm was given and the SAS party succeeded in withdrawing without casualties under enemy mortar fire.

Lieut. Riccomini who was suffering from a septic foot, Pct. Sumptor, and an Italian guide, were left – after the SAS and partisans withdrew from the ambush position – to follow after the main body slowly. The partisans in Codolo were surrounded and six, including Nina, were shot.

Pcts, Everett and Hann who had been sent out to make a recce of our line of march did not succeed in rejoining the main body for some days. Cpl. Johnson and the mules did not make contact with the main body at Coloretta owing to the fact that he was fired upon en route; most of the mule drivers deserted and the bulk of the equipment was lost, including all W/T equipment, rations, rucksacks, and sleeping bags. With the main body were two mules carrying both Vickers guns. Theses were unloaded before the alarm was given and both mules and equipment were captured by the enemy.

At first light the enemy attacked the First Ligurian Div from Pontremoli, Borgo Val di Taro, Bedonia, Varese, Borgeto, and Calice, simultaneously. Captain Walker Brown and party moved to Rio, 546335, arriving at 17.00 hrs. At 17.30 hrs the enemy opened fire on Rio with a 75 mm gun. The party then moved to the foot of Monte Gottero, 561397, where they spent the night.

<u>21 Jan 45</u> At first light the party crossed the summit of Monte Gottero, 1,640 metres, and halfway up met Lieut. Gibbon and Cpl. Ford together with a number of Italians, who all joined the main party which reached Monte Groppo, 564411, at 21.00 hrs. At 23.00 hrs a force of 400 German infantry were reported one hour's march distance. The force of 1,200 partisans, drawn from a number of different bands, which was holding Monte Groppo, immediately vanished into the mountains on hearing this intelligence. Partisans were extremely well armed. The SAS party marched to Boschetto, 620434, where information was received from partisans that the same force of Germans was an hour's march behind. German officers of this force told civilians that they were hunting British parachutists.

<u>22 Jan 45</u> At 07.00 hrs the SAS moved out of Boschetto (Lieut. Gibbon, Cpl. Ford, and the Italians, moving away separately to their own stick base in the Belforte area), and at 08.00 hrs approximately 2,000 Germans attacked Boschetto and captured the partisan leader, Richetta. At 13.00 hrs the SAS party arrived at Buzzo, 609488, and made contact with Sgt. Rookes and his stick, and Cpl. Larley with Lieut. Gibbon's stick less Lieut. Gibbon and Cpl. Ford, Captain Walker Brown's party by this time had completed 59 hours continous marching without rations or rest. The SAS party now consisted of Captain Walker Brown's party and Sgt. Rookes' party. They move into the mountains one hour's march from Buzzo, where twelve hours rest and food were obtained.

<u>23 Jan 45</u> State of alarm. German troops in Buzzo. The SAS stood to.

<u>24 Jan 45</u> State of alarm. Lieut. Leng joined the party.

<u>25 Jan 45</u> 400 Mongol troops move into Buzzo and a partisan gave warning to the SAS that Mongols were moving up to attack them. This proved to be false. However, the SAS party moved to the deserted village of Nola, 619460, two hours' march from Buzzo.

On the night of the 25th Captain Walker Brown, Lieut. Leng, and an Italian guide patrolled Buzzo to ascertain whether the village was clear of enemy or not. The patrol got to within 20 yards of the village when they were fired upon by a Schmeisser pistol and an MG 42 which fired a complete belt at 20 yards range.

<u>26 Jan 45</u> The SAS party remained at Nola in a state of stand-to.

<u>27 Jan 45</u> The area was reported to be clear of the enemy. Captain Walker Brown's party returned to Rossano where the whole troop, less Lieut. Gibbon and Cpl. Ford, concentrated. During the period of the German attack Lieut. Riccomini and Pct. Sumptor were in hiding in the mountains near Torano. Cpl. Johnson, Pcts. Rose, Gargon, Hildage, Hann, Everett, and Major Lett had made contact and were surrounded in Sero by German troops of the 285 Grenadior Battalion who had

come from Genoa. They succeeded in fighting their way out, losing one Italian and one Russian killed and one Italian wounded, who were attached to their party.

28 Jan 45 Lieut. Leng, B.L.O., left the SAS party who dug up the buried rations and ammunition and rested. A party was sent to Arzelato to recover the B set which had been buried by Cpl. Johnson on the 20 Jan. No wireless communication was established.

29 Jan 45 The party rested. No W/T communication.

30 Jan 45 A message requesting resupply was sent blind and was received at base. The drop was requested for DZ "Huntsville" because a German patrol was billeted on DZ "Halifax" and another patrol was 40 minutes march from DZ "Brighton", and the Rossano area was the only comparatively safe base in the area. Signals were put out on DZ "Huntsville".

31 Jan 45 Signals were put out on DZs "Brighton" and "Huntsville" until weather looked impossible.

1 Feb 45 A runner from Lieut. Gibbon reported and was ordered to return to Lieut. Gibbon with written orders instructing him to close on the main body at Borseda, 665259, as quickly as possible.

2 Feb 45 Weather extremely bad with low clouds and mist. At approximately 08.30 hrs a single Dakota ran in over "Huntsville". Emergency signals were immediately put out at Rossano and a party moved off at the double to "Huntsville" to put out the signals. The aircraft flew round for 90 minutes before seeing our signals. Weather conditions were terrible, with thick low clouds lying half-way down the mountains surrounding "Huntsville". Despite this fact the pilot succeeded in recognising the DZ and making a number of exceedingly accurate runs in. The aircraft flew round no fewer than six times inside a high ring of mountains with tops completely obscured, and with little or no safety margin to spare. About two hours later the same aircraft returned and repeated the same performance. Captain Milne, R.A.M.C., dropped from this aircraft at a height of about 350 ft. His parachute took longer than usual to open but he had a gentle landing on the snow.

3 Feb 45 Captain Milne examined Pct. Rose who was sick and unable to move. He advised that Rose should be instructed to make his own way through the lines when he was fit to move.

4 Feb 45 The party waited for rules to move to Borseda.

5 Feb 45 No. 1 Troop, less Lieut. Gibbon and Cpl. Ford, moved to Borseda, leaving Major Lett and Lieut. Leng at Rossano. Sgt. Rookes and his stick were ordered to attack the Aulla – Spezia road at 745188 with Vickers on the night of the 5/6th Feb. Owing to there being no

moon or clouds they found it impossible until the following day.

<u>6 Feb 45</u> Carried out a recce for a mortar attack on Padivarma, 621211, and also for an ambush position.

<u>7 Feb 45</u> Contact was made with a partisan leader named Bucchione who commanded a band of 150 strong. This band had high morale and had done a considerable amount of damage in their area, including raids on Spezia, and they will definitely fight. On the night 7/8th Feb, Sgt. Rookes with one Vickers gun and three Bren guns destroyed 8 enemy vehicles and inflicted a large number of casualties on a party of German troops and mules bivouacking at the side of the road. The remainder of the troop under Captain Walker Brown attacked the Genoa – Spezia road at 618225, destroying two enemy trucks and damaging a third. Casualties were not known. The enemy burnt down two houses at Statano, 745192, and one house at Manzile, 623244, as a reprisal. An Italian runner from Bucchione's band sent to investigate Sgt. Rookes' attack could not get precise information about casualties, but he reported that civilians living in Isola, 745186, on the scene of the attack, said that there were many enemy killed and wounded.

<u>8 Feb 45</u> Attended conference with Bucchione, who advised against carrying out a mortar attack on Padivarma owing to the fact that since the attack on Borgeto all German troops no longer lived in requisitioned billets by themselves but lived in houses occupied by civilians. Therefore, any attack on Padivarma would undoubtedly cause casualties to civilians which, in Bucchione's opinion, would damage Allied popularity.

Lieut. Gibbon and Cpl. Ford joined the party.

<u>9 Feb 45</u> Signals were put out on Borseda DZ but weather was very bad and therefore there was no drop.

<u>10 Feb 45</u> A B25 dropped operational money and comforts. It was then decided to begin withdrawing slowly towards the Allied lines, carrying out a small number of attacks on the way.

The troop split into two parties. The first party under Captain Walker Brown consisted of Troop HQ, Lieut. Gibbon's stick, Sgt. Rookes' stick, 1 Italian, 1 German, and 4 Poles. The second party consisted of Lieut. Riccomini's stick, Sgt. Wright's stick, 1 Frenchman and 2 Poles, under Lieut. Riccomini. The first party moved off at 15.30 hrs and Lieut. Riccomini's party was ordered to follow 24 hours later. The target of the first party was to ambush the Aulla – Spezia road and the Aulla – Reggio road, and that of the second party to mine the Aulla – Spezia road. The first party carried out a night march to Bruscarolo.

<u>11 Feb 45</u> Captain Walker Brown's party crossed the Magra river and the Aulla – Spezia road at 745189. A German patrol was reported to

move past this point at midnight each night. The SAS party crossed at 24.00 hrs and there was no sign of any German patrol. There was a large amount of traffic on the road. It was decided, however, that it was inadvisable to attack a road at a point on the escape route as it might interfere with POW and also with the second party who were to come on later. It was not possible to attack the road to the North as there were enemy patrols reported patrolling from Aulla. It was also not possible to attack the road to the South because the partisans had blown a bridge in the San Stefano area and there was a very large scale enemy reprisal in progress with artillery, mortars and MGs. The Aulla – Reggio road is difficult to attack as it lies in a valley with a long approach march in country affording no cover. It was decided to withdraw completely, and the following factors were taken into consideration:– (i) That the medical officer advised that the men were exceedingly tired. (ii) It had not been possible to get mules across the Magra river with rations and (iii) The men carried two days rations only in the shape of one tin of bully.

<u>12 Feb 45</u> The party reached Vicchette, 789183, and collected guides.

<u>13 Feb 45</u> The party marched to Vinca, 931128 – a long and tiring march across very rough country. Bren guns had to be left with the partisans as, owing to the physical condition of the men, it was not possible for them to carry much on the last stage of the march across Monte Altissimo.

<u>14 Feb 45</u> The party set off at 08.00 hrs for Forno, 942066, where rucksacks were dumped. Carrying only carbines and reserve .300 ammunition, the party proceeded on from Forno at 15.00 hrs. A party of American pilots who had been shot down joined the SAS party. Guides were unwilling to take the party through enemy positions as the night before an enemy mortar had been registering the escape route on the western side of Monte Altissimo, 686029, and an enemy patrol was believed to have laid fresh minefields. However, they were eventually persuaded to go on. It was decided to move through as a fighting patrol and reach the Allied positions at all costs.

The march over Monte Altissimo was exceedingly difficult and tiring. It was pitch black and not possible to use the ordinary mountain track as it was mined. Therefore about 2,000 ft or more had to be climbed at an average slope of about 1 in 4. The pass at the top of Altissimo was reached at about 23.00 hrs. At the same time an enemy mortar carried out a heavy shoot on several points of the track leading through the enemy positions. At 23.30 hrs an enemy patrol of four men was observed moving up the track 100 yards away towards the SAS party. The advance guard got into fire position ready to ambush them but the enemy observed the party and made away into a gully.

<u>15 Feb 45</u> At 03.00 hrs one of the party sprang an enemy trip wire which ignited a white phosphorous flare. It was thought that this was

a signal for defensive fire but nothing happened.

At 04.00 hrs the party passed the forward American platoon.

APPENDICES

(a) PARTISAN ACTIVITY AND POLITICS

In the area of the First Ligurian Division partisans morale is very low and organisation poor. With a few exceptions they will not fight and were most uneasy when the S.A.S. party arrived. The exceptions are the following:-

> Band of Bucchione
> Band of Richetta
> Cento Croce Brigade

These have a good reputation and will probably fight. The vast majority of other partisan formations are largely interested in getting food and clothing from Allied resupply drops and little else. Communist bands are causing trouble and have sent complaints to the Committees of Liberation, Colonel "Turki", and Major Lett, complaining against what they describe as the "Allied influence" in their area. Major Lett, B.L.O., is convinced that, given a chance, the Communists will put a round through him. The S.A.S. party was refused assistance in the shape of men for an attack by the Communist Justice and Liberty Brigade of Pieve. On the 9th January 1945 a party of Justice and Liberty Communists fired on the DZ "Halifax" during a drop. Later the same party attempted to loot S.A.S. food and cigarettes from the DZ. Captain Walker Brown ordered Pct. Gargan to fire two rounds from a pistol into the air. Communists ran back two hundred yards and opened fire on the S.A.S. with Sten guns and rifles. S.A.S. replied by firing two Bren magazines above their heads very low and a third into their midst as they ran away. No casualties were inflicted on them. The S.A.S. avoided operating with partisans owing to their complete unreliability.

A more detailed report on partisans will be submitted by Lieut. Riccomini who speaks fluent Italian and carried out most of the liaison with the partisans.

(b) WEATHER CONDITIONS

The influence of weather on this operation was very considerable. For about four weeks the mountains and valleys were covered in deep snow, frequently waist or thigh deep, and the mountain tracks were covered in packed snow turned to ice. At times mules took as much as over two hours to cover a mile and men were in a constant state of fatigue. Waiting several days at a time for resupply, made impossible by bad weather, was the most considerable factor in hindering more intensive action.

(c) RATIONS

Bully beef, though sustaining, becomes very monotonous, and

therefore men do not derive full benefit from their food.

It is suggested that in future, owing to the difficulty of obtaining fresh food from the land, the following should be included in resupply rations:-

> Arctic Rations.
> Compo Rations.
> K Rations.
> Greens.
> Apples, dried or fresh.
> Oranges.
> Larger quantities of flour.

(d) NOTES ON EQUIPMENT

In the troop area all heavy stores had to be carried by mules. It is not possible to do long carries with a 3″ mortar or a Vickers MMG for more than 1,000 yards.

The British 3″ HV Mortar has a maximum range of 2,700 yards, normally sufficient for attacking a single target but not for carrying out switches against widely separated targets. The Italian 81 mm mortar model 35 has a range of 4,300 metres and is about the same weight as the British 3″ mortar, i.e. 140 lbs. It is suggested that this is a more suitable weapon.

The Vickers MMG was used with success. It is an ideal weapon to use in conjunction with a 3″ mortar.

Had trained gunners been available it would have been possible to use a 3.7″ mountain gun.

Finnish pattern boots were nearly all worn out after 3 weeks marching. A stronger type of boot is needed.

There was a shortage of trained mortar numbers and Vickers machine gunners. The only trained mortar numbers were Captain Walker Brown and Pct. Rose. The only trained machine gunners were Sgt. Rookes and Cpl. Larley. A 2″ mortar with parachute flare bombs was requested. This would have been of great value in night ambushes on moonless nights.

Snow suits should have been dropped when the troop disemplaned. Men in khaki or jumping smocks stand out for miles against a background of snow and concealment is virtually impossible.

(e) LESSONS LEARNT

1. Combined mortar and machine gun attacks against enemy held towns seem to produce more rapid and heavy reaction than simple ambushing of roads. In addition, enemy traffic was invariably halted for a considerable number of hours after one of

these attacks.

2. A high standard of physical fitness is required before dropping troops who have to march long distances in mountainous country. Men should invariably carry on their bodies at all times the following:

> Sleeping bag.
> Windproof jacket.
> Spare nails for boots
> One tin of bully, or equivalent.
> Medical pack.

3. In withdrawing from an ambush position under fire and up difficult country it is essential that both number one and number two on the Bren assist each other in carrying the gun.

4. It was found that 1/25,000 maps were invaluable for estimating the ranges for Vickers MG and 3" mortar. The maximum weight men can carry across snow covered mountainous country is 20 lbs in their packs. If heavier weights are carried men become excessively fatigued.

5. Mules are essential for carrying heavy stores but they cannot be taken closer than 800 yards to the fire position owing to the amount of noise they make on rough rocky tracks.

6. Some form of overshoe with rubber soles to fit over mountain boots is very necessary owing to the fact that when men ascend or, particularly, descend steep, boulder strewn tracks heavily nailed shoes continually slip on rocks, causing a loud screeching noise and occasional sparks.

7. Tobacco, coffee, salt and flour, as bargaining mediums have greater value than money.

8. The area is full of spies and it is vital that troops should not make obvious preparation to leave until the latest possible moment when under observation by Italians, or mention any place names remotely connected with targets or places on the line of march. Even pointing to places on maps should be avoided. To quote an example: Before the troop attacked the Pontremoli – Aulla road on the night of the 19 Jan, despite the fact that the SAS column left Arzelato in total darkness the enemy garrison at Pontremoli was warned of our approach and was in a state of stand-to ten minutes after we had left.

9. When using the 3" mortar it is essential that all personnel should be warned that any movement around, towards or away from the mortar, will reveal its position. The range of the 3" mortar can be increased by sitting it as high as possible above the target. All

mortar ammunition should not be unloaded from the mules at the beginning of the attack in case a quick withdrawal is to be carried out. Owing to the large amount of movement necessary in mounting the mortar, carrying up of ammunition and establishing observation posts, the mortar should be in position and ready to fire before first light. No civilians or partisans must be allowed to pass the mortar or Vickers position if they are proceeding in the direction of enemy, unless the time factor would obviously make it impossible to warn the enemy.

10. To produce sufficient fire power there should not normally be less than a group of three Brens, one of which should not open fire until the other two are changing magazines.

11. Italian guides should be accompanied by a British soldier on reaching an attack position as they usually run away when fire is opened.

12. Owing to the considerable distances at which observation is carried out 6 x 30 binoculars should be replaced by 7 x 50 which are not much heavier and three times as efficient.

13. When more than ten men are on the move it is essential that a small patrol of one guide and two men should be placed forward at least half a mile. Therefore, two guides who know the route should always be taken. (One guide for the patrol and one for the main body.)

14. Troops should be practiced in passing verbal messages down the column. Odd bodies such as Italian porters should be at the tail of the column otherwise messages cannot be passed back quickly from the head.

(f) RESUPPLY

Invariably aircraft dropped too many containers on each run in. The result is that stores get spread over too large an area and it is impossible to control pilfering by partisans and civilians. Maximum of five containers or packages should be dropped on each run in. Parachutes, blankets or sheets are often difficult to obtain. White or coloured smoke generators should be available for signals. Ground signals should only be put out when the aircraft is observed, and should be changed frequently as partisans have copied signals in order to mislead the aircraft and obtain a drop.

Monte San Martino Trust

I have been greatly assisted whilst researching this book by the Monte San Martino Trust and, as the Epilogue outlines, I have been on several of their fund-raising expeditions to Italy whilst researching my father's war-time exploits during SAS Operation Galia.

The Trust was founded by former POWs to repay some of their debt to Italian families who helped, sheltered, fed and, in many cases, guided them (and other escapees) to safety during the Second World War.

For twenty years the Trust has provided bursaries to young Italians to give them a chance to study English in the UK. About a third of the students are descendants of the *Contadini* families who assisted the POWs.

The Trust maintains an archive of manuscripts of former POWs and organises 'freedom trails' for anyone interested in history and/or the relatives of the POWs following the routes that their fathers and grandfathers took while on the run in various parts of occupied Italy.

The Trust relies heavily on donations to fund the cost of the annual bursaries to Italian students. Bequests through wills can be made to include the charity as a beneficiary. Such bequests are not only advantageous from the point of view of inheritance tax, but can easily and economically be arranged by means of a codicil.

Contact the Trust Treasurer Nicholas Gent for further details via the web site: www.msmtrust.org.uk

Bibliography

Brookes, Thomas R. (2003) *The War North of Rome June 1944–May 1945*, Sarpedon.

Darman, Peter (1997) *A-Z Guide of the SAS*, Sidgwick and Jackson.

Farran, Roy (1998) *Winged Dagger: Adventures on Special Service*, Cassel Military Classics.

Gibbon, Lieutenant Edward 'Tinkler' (2003) *Voice Recording*, Imperial War Museum.

Holland, James (2008) *Italy's Sorrow; A Year of War 1944–45*, Harper Press.

Kemp, Anthony (2000) *The SAS at War 1941–45*, John Murray.

Lett, Brian SAS in Tuscany, Pen and Sword

Lett, Gordon (1955) *Rossano: An Adventure of the Italian Resistance*, Hodder and Stoughton.

Lucas, James (1999) *Hitler's Mountain Troops*, Arms and Armour Press.

Mondey, David (1994) *The Concise Guide to American Aircraft of World War II*, Chancellor Press.

Mortimer, Gavin (2004) *Stirling's Men: The Inside History of the SAS in World War II*, Orion Books.

Reid, Howard (2004) *Dad's War*, Bantam Press.

Shirer, William (1990) *The Rise and Fall of the Third Reich*, Secker-Warburg.

Stolley, Richard (2005) *World War II in Pictures*, Life, Time-Warner.

Walker Brown, Captain Bob 1944/5 *The Operational Order and Debrief Report of Operation Galia*, Unpublished.

Walker Brown, Captain Bob, *Briefing Notes of Workshop to 22nd SAS 1997*, Unpublished.

Walker Brown, Captain Bob, *Voice Recording*, Imperial War Museum.

Warner, Philip (1983) *The SAS: The Official History*, Sphere Books.

Photographs

3 Squadron 2 SAS

Reviews of Galia on Amazon:

5 out of 5 stars excellent, *Mr. Pj Williams (Cardiff UK)*

finally got round to reading this as it has been on my shelf for ages and funnily enough I was in Italy when I read it following the trail of my grandfather on operation tombola (not to far away). well on reading it I can say its very well researched (its incredibly difficult trying to put these actions into order of how they happened and the members involved) in its descriptions of the real events, and its inclusion of back round information concerning what lead to the mission. what really helps is the authors narrative style. He writes it in the voice of his father, which at first I had my doubts about as I never like to cross fact with fiction but he has only it seems included stories told by his father into the book conversationally that don't impact on the history, which to me is subtle excellence as the temptation to spice it up must have been hard to ignore. all in all a great book to add to the sas collection, and a great piece of research for family members to obtain for their research. only downside is no index but that is a publishers prerogative so no loss in rating for me look forward to his next work

5 out of 5 stars Gripping, realistic...a masterpiece,
Lord Richard A. McKenzie-Browne

This has to be one of the best reads I have ever had. The realism in prose, attention to detail and the vast amount of research involved is a true credit to the Author. I could not put this book down and almost felt myself present with the heroes of the Galia campaign. Hann writes with meticulous precision, hard hitting and inspiring. Well deserved five stars....well worthy of documentary/film status.

5 out of 5 stars *By TOMMO "A PILGRIM" (PORTSMOUTH)*

Could not put this book down wonderfully written
well done to Robert Hann the way he gets into the story is wonderful
I really recommend this book to anyone interested in world war2 and the regiment .
I salute you and may you write many more like it first class

Brings a little-known chapter of WWII history vividly to life. Gripping.
5 out of 5 stars *By D. G. Rowles (Isle of Wight, UK)*

I couldn't put this book down. I think it is an absolute must for WWII fans.
Well done to the author for such meticulous research to bring us a unique perspective on an unusual and truly heroic story which might otherwise have gone untold. You can't claim to know about WWII until you have read this heart-felt account. Five stars. Maybe one day would make a great film.

Genuine insight into an SAS WW2 operation in Italy
By R. G. Barlow (Nottingham UK)

This is a fascinating account of SAS WW2 activity behind enemy lines in Northern Italy. The author has taken great care to research the detail which he uses to illustrate the account of the Operation.

There is substantial poignancy in the circumstances which the SAS encountered when so many innocent Italians were killed by the facists and germans in reprisals and also in the author's own story about his father who decided never to tell his son of his bravery and wartime experience.

I can thoroughly recommend this book as a real insight into the wartime achievement of the SAS and its effect upon the northern Italian community.